A Short Introduction to the Study of Language

A Short Introduction to the Study of Language

Ellen Thompson

SHEFFIELD UK   BRISTOL CT

Published by Equinox Publishing Ltd

UK: Office 415, The Workstation, 15 Paternoster Row, Sheffield, South Yorkshire S1 2BX

USA: ISD, 70 Enterprise Drive, Bristol, CT 06010

www.equinoxpub.com

First published 2019

British Library Cataloguing-in-Publication Data

A catalogue record for this book is available from the British Library.

ISBN-13 978 1 78179 772 3 (hardback)

978 1 78179 773 0 (paperback)

978 1 78179 774 7 (ePDF)

Library of Congress Cataloging-in-Publication Data

Names: Thompson, Ellen, 1967- author.

Title: A short introduction to the study of language / Ellen Thompson.

Description: Sheffield, South Yorkshire ; Bristol, CT : Equinox Publishing
    Ltd., [2019] | Includes bibliographical references.

Identifiers: LCCN 2018012863 (print) | LCCN 2018042801 (ebook) | ISBN
    9781781797747 (ePDF) | ISBN 9781781797723 | ISBN 9781781797723 q(hb) |
    ISBN 9781781797730 q(pb) | ISBN 9781781797747 q(ePDF)

Subjects: LCSH: Language and languages--Study and teaching. | Languages,
    Modern--Study and teaching. | Language acquisition.

Classification: LCC PB35 (ebook) | LCC PB35 .T526 2019 (print) | DDC
    418.0071--dc23

LC record available at https://lccn.loc.gov/2018012863

Typeset by Steve Barganski

Printed and bound in the UK by Lightning Source UK Ltd, Milton Keynes and Lightning Source Inc., La Vergne, TN

I dedicate this book to my children, Mariam Nassirnia and Mirza Amin Nassirnia, for the nyawins and wagigs. Thank you for making my life wonderful every day.

Contents

Preface

I am very happy to write these words of thanks to so many people who contributed to the evolution of this book. I wish to thank the English Department and the Latin American and Caribbean Center at Florida International University for their generous support of my work. In particular, I am indebted to my chair Heather Russell for her tremendous kindness and encouragement.

To my generous colleagues, a huge thank you is due for coffee, wine, and putting things into perspective: Craig McGill, Ana Luscynska, Lynn Berk, Carmela McIntyre, Heather Blatt, Kimberly Harrison, Martha Schoolman, Jamie Sutton, and Rhona Trauvitch. A big shout out to my fellow FIU Linguists: Phillip Carter, Tomi Hopkins, Melissa Baralt, and Bennett Schwartz, for being terrific colleagues. Thank you to Natasha Neckles and Gretter Manchin for their constant and generous support.

I owe a ton of gratitude and huge hugs to my family: Mary Lally Thompson, Mary Thompson, Ruth Thompson, Richard Thompson, Cathy Thompson, Altea Paz Thompson, Wilem Thompson, Ella Thompson, and Aunt Tan. Thank you for always being there for me.

For crucial intervention, I extend my warmest hugs to the batas: Lorena Zito, Pia Robalino, and Gigi Hernandez. I couldn't make it through the day without you. For long-distance hugs, I am grateful to Marcela Depiante and Jairo Nunes.

Also, I need to thank Ted Chiang for inspiration and a last burst of energy. Gina Alaijian is owed a huge debt of gratitude for assistance with putting together this book. I am especially grateful to Fatima for her continued patience and kindness.

Thank you to the editors of Equinox Publishing for being a pleasure to work with.

CHAPTER 1

What is Language?

1.1 Introduction

Widespread the this of language and provides study introduction book an to language and number myths a of misconceptions explores about. Why does this sentence sound odd as the first sentence of a book about language? Perhaps it is because this string of words does not sound like a sentence at all, but just a jumbled up bunch of words. If we were to reconfigure these words as, "This book provides an introduction to the study of language, and explores a number of widespread myths and misconceptions about language," then we would have something closer to what we expect at the beginning of a book. But what is it precisely about our first "sentence" that makes it not a sentence? What are the unconscious rules and processes that make it possible for us to distinguish between natural-sounding and unnatural-sounding sentences?

It does not seem to be something that we learned in school, since if we were to say the first "sentence" to someone who knows how to speak but not read English, their reaction would be the same as ours. So it seems to be something that we know as speakers of English that is part of our unconscious knowledge of the language. In fact, we will see that some of the most complex and interesting properties of language are those that we know and apply without being aware of them.

In order to get a glimpse into the world of language, I will discuss topics that are of wide interest, and sometimes heated debate. I will ask the following questions:

- Is English getting worse (or better)?
- How do children and adults learn language?
- Do all languages have grammars?
- Is human language different from other animal communication systems?
- How do bilinguals learn two languages?

The purpose of this book is to bring to your attention the work that linguists are engaged in today which explores these questions, as well as many other fascinating questions about human language.

1.2 Creativity of Human Language

Linguists are interested in understanding the structure and use of human language. One of the defining properties of language is that it is creative—as speakers of a language, we have the ability to understand sentences that we have never heard before, and to create new sentences that may have never been spoken. For example, I may say (1.1):

(1.1)

> The last contestant on the show confused the five-thousand camels who were busy relaxing beach-side on the Riviera.

You may consider this to be an unlikely sentence, and in fact it is possible that no one in the history of the English language has ever uttered this sentence. Nevertheless, if you are a speaker of English, you will be able to understand this sentence, and you will be able to create readily your own new sentences that may have never been created in the history of English.

When linguists speak of the creativity of human language, they are thus referring to this key property of every speaker of a language to use the language in new and unpredictable ways—this contrasts with the way in which "the creativity of human language" may be understood in terms of the poetic or artistic use of language.

1.3 Infinite Capacity of Language

It seems that there is no limit to the complexity of the sentences that we may in principle utter or understand, since for every sentence that exists, there is a way to make that sentence more complex. Consider the sentence in (1.2):

(1.2)

The boss is busy.

By placing this sentence inside a larger sentence, we can form:

(1.3)

The assistant believes that the boss is busy.

And this sentence may in turn be placed into a still-larger sentence:

(1.4)

Mariam reported that the assistant believes that the boss is busy.

Another way in which sentences may become more complex is shown if we start with the same sentence as (1.2), repeated in (1.5), and make it more complex by adding another sentence, *He is getting impatient*, to the end of this sentence with the conjunction *and*, as in (1.6):

(1.5)

The boss is busy.

(1.6)

The boss is busy, and he is getting impatient.

To this sentence we may add still more material, as in (1.7):

(1.7)

The boss is busy, and he is getting impatient, but he will leave the office at exactly 5:00 p.m.

We may continue to add more structure, as in (1.8):

(1.8)
> The boss is busy, and he is getting impatient, but he will leave the office at exactly 5:00 p.m. and he will show up again tomorrow at 9:00 a.m.

For every sentence of English, we can create a still-longer version of that sentence. In terms of actually producing a very complex sentence, if we were to attempt to produce a sentence that has 5,000 words in it, we would probably get pretty tired of doing this after the first 20 words or so. However, in principle there is no longest sentence of English; the number of English sentences is infinite.

1.4 The Rules of English Grammar

How is it possible that we have a limited number of words in English, and yet the number of sentences that we can create with these words is unlimited? The reason that we can use human language in this way is that, as speakers of English, we use a system of rules to create sentences and these rules may be applied repeatedly to form new sentences.

In this respect, our knowledge of language is similar to our knowledge of numbers. In principle there is no limit to the numbers that you may list: 1, 2, 3, 4, etc. In this sense you know an infinite list of numbers. But of course you did not memorize all these numbers—you know a rule that allows you to produce new numbers from old ones. The rule is: for any number N, N + 1 is another number.

In a similar way, it is the rules of English that tell us it is possible to form an English sentence by saying, for example, (1.9):

(1.9)
> I love Mirza's oatmeal cookies.

It is also possible to change the sentence in (1.9) to form the sentence in (1.10), because we have a rule in English which allows us to place the object of the verb at the front of the sentence to emphasize it:

(1.10)

Mirza's oatmeal cookies, I love.

However, notice that the possibilities for moving the words of the sentence around are limited—if we try to change *I love Mirza's oatmeal cookies* to the sentence in (1.11), this does not sound like a possible sentence of English.

(1.11)

*Oatmeal love Mirza's I cookies.

The sentence in (1.11) is preceded by a star (*) to show that it is not a possible sentence of English—any sentence which does not sound to English speakers like a normal sentence is marked in this way. The goal of describing English sentences is to explain why some sentences are possible while others are impossible.

1.5 Descriptive versus Prescriptive Grammar

We have thus far been discussing the rules of English in terms of describing what it is that speakers of English do when they speak and understand the language. However, you may be familiar with another approach to language rules—the prescriptive approach. The distinction between prescriptive rules and descriptive rules is key to understanding the goals of modern linguistics (Crystal, 2010; Chomsky, 1965).

Prescriptive rules are intended to teach people how they should speak or write according to a predetermined, arbitrary standard. Prescriptive rules have no relevance for the scientific study of language, since linguists are interested in describing and understanding the rules that speakers do in fact follow. Think of linguistics in relation to botany, the study of plant life. Botanists are interested in describing and explaining the various forms of plant life that exist in the world; however, they would not attempt to give advice about the ways in which plants should grow or the behavior, size, or reproductive life of plants.

Most of us are familiar with prescriptive language rules from learning them in school, and have at some point been corrected for using sentences which do not follow these rules. In the following section, we will discuss several prescriptive rules and then return to a discussion of the descriptive rules of English.

1.5.1 Prescriptive Rules of English Grammar
1.5.1.1 Do not End a Sentence with a Preposition
An example of a prescriptive rule of English grammar is: "Do not end a sentence with a preposition." According to this rule, we should not say (1.12), since the sentence ends with the preposition *from*:

(1.12)

Where are you from?

Instead, we should say the sentence as in (1.13):

(1.13)

From where are you?

Notice that it would sound very unnatural for most speakers of English to say the sentence as in (1.13); the normal way to say the sentence would be as in (1.12). In fact, Winston Churchill was reportedly once corrected for using a sentence that did not follow these rules, and he poked fun at the rules by responding (1.14) (Zimmer, 2004):

(1.14)

This is the kind of stuff up with which I will not put.

Churchill produced this sentence in order to show how odd it sounds to follow the prescriptive rule of English not to end a sentence with a preposition, as the natural English sentence in (1.15) does:

(1.15)

This is the kind of stuff which I will not put up with.

You may then wonder where this rule came from (or, from where this rule came). Bishop Robert Lowth (1710–1787) is the author of the 1762 book *A Short Introduction to English Grammar*, in which he introduces many prescriptive rules for English, including the prohibition against ending a sentence with a preposition. In fact, Lowth uses that very construction in his condemnation of it: "This is an Idiom which our language is strongly inclined to; but the placing of the Preposition before the Relative is more graceful, as well as more perspicuous; and agrees much better with the solemn and elevated Style."

As were most grammarians at his time, Lowth was trained in the classical languages Latin and Greek, and considered these ancient languages to be more logical and expressive than English. Grammarians were therefore intent on "improving" English by making it more like Latin and Greek. In Latin, it is not possible to produce a sentence with a preposition at the end. We can see this by looking at this type of sentence in a language that descends directly from Latin—Spanish.

If you are a speaker of Spanish, translate the sentence *Where are you from?* into Spanish. Notice that the form of the sentence is different than it is in English. Spanish speakers would say (1.16), and would not produce the sentence as in (1.17):

(1.16)

¿De	donde	eres?
From	where	are-you

"Where are you from?"

(1.17)

*¿Donde	eres	de?
Where	are-you	from

"Where are you from?"

Spanish speakers do not learn in school not to produce sentences that end in a preposition like (1.17); regardless of whether a person has attended school or not, they produce the sentence as in (1.16). If a speaker of Spanish heard the sentence in (1.17), they would understand what the sentence means; it would sound perhaps like someone who is learning Spanish and is getting the words right but not the order.

Many of the prescriptive rules of English grammar are based on attempts to make English more like Latin. However, modern linguistics claims that all human languages are logical and expressive, and therefore no language can be said to be superior to any other language. We are thus interested in describing how speakers of English use the language, and not in telling speakers how they should use the language.

1.5.1.2 Do not Use Double Negatives

Another prescriptive rule that you are probably familiar with is: "Do not use two negatives in the same sentence." In other words, do not say a sentence as in (1.18a), but instead say it as in (1.18b):

(1.18)
   a.   I didn't see nothing.
   b.   I didn't see anything.

The logic of this rule is claimed to be that "Two negatives equals a positive," so if you say, "I didn't see nothing," you are actually expressing, "I saw something." Notice that the concept of two negatives equaling a positive is from mathematics, where it does hold true. The classical grammarians of the eighteenth century, trained in mathematics and wishing to impose a logical system on to what they considered to be the "unruly" and "exception-filled" language of English, thus modeled English grammar on the system of mathematics.

However, is it the case that the rules of language are the same as the rules of mathematics? Math is concerned with the study of quantity, structure, and space, and therefore the rules of mathematics are appropriate to describing these phenomena. Human language, on the other hand, is the vehicle for the expression of thought. Therefore, there does not seem to be any reason to think that these areas of human knowledge will share the same rules.

We can see that the prescriptive rule of English against double negatives is arbitrary by examining these structures in other languages. If you are a speaker of Spanish or French, translate the sentence in (1.19) into that language:

(1.19)

I didn't see anything.

If you translated into Spanish, you would have something like (1.20):

(1.20)

No	*vi*	*nada.*
Not	saw I	nothing

"I didn't see anything."

The literal translation of this into English is "I didn't see nothing," a sentence with two negatives: *no* and *nada*. Notice that when a speaker of Spanish says, "No vi nada," there is no confusion about whether the speaker means "I didn't see anything" or "I saw something"—the sentence has only the negative meaning. However, if it were a rule of logic in using language that "two negatives equals a positive," we would expect all languages to follow this rule.

In fact, linguists have noted that what is considered grammatically proper depends on historical circumstances that have nothing to do with purely linguistic or logical considerations. For instance, in contemporary French, double negation is considered to be "proper," while single negation is considered "sloppy"—the opposite pattern from the one we find in English:

(1.21)

a. Contemporary French—Prestige Dialect

Il	*ne*	*mange*	*rien.*
he	not	eats	nothing

"He doesn't eat anything."

b. Contemporary French—Colloquial Language

Il	*mange*	*rien.*
he	eats	nothing

"He doesn't eat anything."

The sentence from the more prestigious dialect in (1.21a) includes the two negative words, *ne* and *rien*, while the sentence in (1.21b) from the low-prestige form of French uses one negative word, *rien*.

It is important to note that double negatives, found in many contemporary non-standard dialects of English, are not a recent innovation in the language, but have existed for centuries. In Chaucer's *Canterbury Tales*, written at the end of the 14th century, we find the lines in (1.22):

(1.22)

Curteis he was and lowely of servyse.

Ther nas **no** man **nowher** so virtuous.

"Courteous he was and humble in service.

There was **no** man **nowhere** so virtuous."

William Shakespeare, the most revered author in the English language, makes use of multiple negatives, as in the example in (1.23), from Act III, Scene 1 of *Twelfth Night* (1601–1602):

(1.23a)

By innocence I swear, and by my youth

I have one heart, one bosom and one truth,

And that no woman has; nor never none

Shall mistress be of it, save I alone.

We might "translate" the last two lines above into contemporary English as:

(1.23b)

And that no woman has; and no woman

will ever be mistress of it, except for me alone.

1.5.1.3 Do not Split Infinitives

The rule against split infinitives dictates that we should not say (1.24a), but instead (1.24b):

(1.24)

a.   I wanted to slowly eat the spaghetti that Mary had made.

b.   I wanted to eat the spaghetti slowly that Mary had made.

Since grammarians in the past modeled English grammar on Latin, this rule is based on the equivalent structure in Latin. In Latin, since the infinitive is a single word (e.g. *manducare*) as it is in contemporary Romance languages such as Spanish *comer* and French *manger*, it is not possible to break it up with an adverb.

Contemporary linguists conclude that, since no language is superior to any other language, there is no reason for English to behave like Latin. In English, *to eat* is made of two words, not one, and therefore there is no reason for an adverb to not come between them.

1.6 Is Colloquial English "Sloppy"?

According to proponents of prescriptive grammar, the written, formal version of English is superior to the colloquial, "sloppy," spoken form of the language. However, if we examine in detail examples of what are considered sloppy speech or slang, we see that all of these forms are in fact governed by systematic, linguistically complex rules. (See Finegan, 2005 and Fought, 2005 for discussion of prescriptivist and descriptivist views on language.)

1.6.1 Expletive Infixation in English

Colloquial English has a process of expletive emphasis which is illustrated in (1.25). (We would not expect to find examples like this in formal written English.)

(1.25)

  I wanna buy that house so fricking bad.

The meaning of *fricking* (or other expletives) is to intensify another word, similar to other intensifying words such as *very*. (Notice that *I wanna buy that house so very bad* doesn't carry the same feeling as the original.)

It is possible to insert the expletive in colloquial English *inside* of a word as well, as shown in (1.26a) and (1.26b), although this is not possible with other (non-expletive) intensifiers, as shown in (1.27a) and (1.27b). The insertion of a word into another word is what we call "infixation."

(1.26)

   a.   He is fricking intense.

   b.   He is in-fricking-tense.

(1.27)

   a.   He is very intense.

   b.   *He is in-very-tense.

We can alter the following sentence so that it has this type of infixation, where (1.28a) is the original sentence and (1.28b) has expletive-infixation inside of a word:

(1.28)

   a.   That guy is fricking fantastic.

   b.   That guy is fan-fricking-tastic.

The interesting linguistic point is that although we could have said *fan-fricking-tastic*, we would all agree that neither of the versions in (1.29a–b) would be acceptable:

(1.29)

   a.   *That guy is fantas-fricking-tic.

   b.   *That guy is fantast-fricking-ic.

The fact that an odd result is obtained when *fricking* is inserted in incorrect positions indicates that this process is systematic. The descriptive rule for this process is that expletive infixation in English may occur only before a syllable which receives primary stress in the word. (The prescriptive rule for this process would be something like, "Do not say this.")

Let us see how this works for our example:

(1.30)

That guy is fan-fricking-tastic.

The word *fantastic* is made up of three syllables: *fan-tas-tic*. The syllable that receives the most stress in the word (primary stress) is *tas*, and thus expletive infixation may occur in the position before *tas*: *fan-fricking-tastic*.

What we can conclude from examining the process of expletive insertion in English is that this rule of colloquial English, although considered by prescriptivists to be an example of "bad usage", is, in fact, a structurally complex and hence expected rule of language. In fact, there are many languages which have a rule for infixation which follows patterns similar to this one.

Bontoc is one such language. Spoken in the Philippines, this language makes use of infixation as well. Examine the data from Bontoc below and consider the analysis of these words (examples are adapted from Fromkin, Rodman, & Hyams, 2014, p. 41):

(1.31)

Adjective		Verb	
pusi	"poor"	*pumusi*	"to be poor"
fusul	"enemy"	*fumusul*	"to be an enemy"
fanig	"small"	*fumanig*	"to be small"
fikas	"strong"	*fumikas*	"to be strong"
kilad	"red"	*kumilad*	"to be red"

The first question that we have here is what is going on with the change of a word like *pusi* "poor", to *pumusi* "to be poor". It looks like the adjective for *poor* in Bontoc can change into a verb, *to be poor*. Notice that English has something like this as well, shown in the word *regularize*. *Regularize* is a verb, since it can appear with the past tense marker and refer to an action as in, "The boss regularized the system." But the word *regular* in English is an adjective—it is used to modify a noun, as in "the regular routine." So in English we can begin with the adjective *regular* and turn it into a verb by adding *-ize* onto the end. Thus, in English we add something to the end of a word to change that word into a verb, whereas Bontoc adds something to the inside of a word to do the same thing.

Let us state how verbs are made from adjectives in Bontoc. The infix *um* appears after the first consonant in the word—we can express this as, "After the first consonant in an adjective, add *um* to the word to make it into a verb."

1.7 Language Rules are Unconscious

Notice that, as a speaker of English, you are constantly making use of your knowledge of English grammar without being aware of it. As you are reading this sentence, you are extracting the meaning of the sentence without thinking to yourself, "Okay, this is the first Noun Phrase of the clause, so I'll analyze this as the subject of the sentence, and then this must be the beginning of the predicate ..." We immediately, effortlessly, and automatically make use of the abstract rules of English every time we speak or understand a sentence of English. The creative use of abstract linguistic structure is exemplified in the work of George Orwell, who has introduced many new words to the English language, including *chortle*. The word is a blend of *chuckle* and *snort* (similar to the word *brunch*, which is made up of *breakfast* and *lunch*). *Chortle* refers to the sound made when someone laughs and at the same time uses their nose in the process. The author George Orwell need not have been engaged in abstract linguistic analysis of the structure of English in order to coin new words—as a speaker of English, he was able to create words which followed the complex linguistic rules of his language.

Notice that this process of introducing new words into English is ongoing: we hear new words and learn new expressions quite commonly. Consider the following examples of new English words:

(1.32)

  a.   chillax
  b.   affluenza
  c.   bromance
  d.   cronut
  e.   crowdfunding
  f.   cyberbully

The word *chillax*, as in "Mark has been chillaxing in his room all day," is made up of the two words *chill* and *relax*. The word refers to the state of being calmed down and relaxed. It has this meaning because it is a combination of *chill* and *relax.*

What are the parts of the word *affluenza*? An example of this is: "Attorneys argued that the teen suffered from affluenza since he did not know right from wrong due to his wealthy upbringing." It seems that *affluence* plus *influenza* combine to give us this word. The meaning is derived from the two parts; it refers to a type of sickness (influenza), here, a negative social effect, such as feelings of social isolation and guilt, that are due to material wealth (affluence). Take a look at the rest of the words in (1.32) to see if you can determine what the parts of the word are and how they come together to form the meaning of the new word. Just as we can form new sentences in English, we thus can form new words as well.

Note that we may become aware of the complex processes of English if someone who is learning English asks us, "Why can't I say, 'John not left the room'?; Why do I have to say, 'John didn't leave the room'?" In some instances, your response to questions like this might be, "...", or the equally insightful, "Because you just can't say it that way in English." Linguists aim to discover what the abstract knowledge is that all speakers of a language have, and are thereby making conscious and analyzing what we already inherently know. So if you would like to be able to say in response to such a question, "Because the rule for sentential negation in English requires that the first auxiliary verb of the main clause appear with the negative clitic *n't* attached to it, and if the sentence does not have an auxiliary verb, then the auxiliary verb *do* is inserted and takes the inflection of the main verb, thus becoming *did*, and turning *left* into *leave*," then continue reading this book.

Suggested Materials and Resources

To learn more about linguistics, the Ling Space provides a forum for discussion of all topics related to linguistics and language: http://www.thelingspace.com

The International Linguistics Olympiad is a competition that is held annually and is one of twelve Science International Olympiads. The ILO website provides information about participating, as well as examples of previous years' linguistics problems. http://www.ioling.org/participation/#by_country

If you would like to take a free introductory course in linguistics online, there are courses offered through the following site: https://www.coursera.org/learn/human-language

For an exciting introduction to work on the language documentation of endangered languages, see the film *The Linguists*: Kramer, Miller, and Newberger (2009).

Lightfoot (1982) and Long and Ross (2011) provide accessible introductions to Noam Chomsky's ideas.

Several excellent introductions to Noam Chomsky's theory of generative grammar which is adopted in this book can be found in Hornstein and Lightfoot (1981), Uriagereka (1998), Haegeman (2006), and Radford (2016).

CHAPTER 2

Language and Other Animal Communication Systems

> Human language appears to be a unique phenomenon, without significant analogue in the animal world.
>
> Noam Chomsky (1972)

2.1 Introduction

Linguists are interested in understanding if language is a uniquely human ability. Is human language significantly different from other animal communication systems, or is it just one more example of a sophisticated animal communication system? The answer to this question depends on our definition of language.

The Cambridge English Dictionary defines language as "a system of communication by speaking, writing, or making signs in a way that can be understood." According to this definition, we may want to say that many non-human animals do possess language. For example, as will be discussed later in this chapter, bees have a system of communication whereby a dance that the forager bee does indicates to the other bees of the hive the location and quality of the food source. This certainly qualifies as a system of communication that can be understood.

However, the more precise question that linguists have in mind in comparing human language to other animal communication systems is whether these systems are significantly like human language—do they have the defining properties that human languages have, or are they different in kind from human languages?

Scientists have explored this issue in two different ways: they have asked, "Do animal communication systems have the uniquely defining properties of human language?", and they have asked, "Can non-human animals be taught human language?" In this chapter, we will examine the work that linguists have done to investigate the first of these questions, and in Chapter 3, we will explore research on the second one.

Linguists have attempted to discover the features which all human languages, no matter how historically or typologically distinct, necessarily share. We may then ask whether these are features that other animal communication systems possess.

2.2 What Makes Human Language Special?

2.2.1 Defining Properties of Human Language

The linguist Charles Hockett (1960, 1967) proposed a list of design features of human language and claimed that, while animal communication systems may have some of these design features, only human language has all of them:

1.	Vocal-auditory channel	Human language is made up of sounds which are perceived by the hearer.
2.	Broadcast transmission and directional reception	The sounds of spoken language go out in all directions, but they are perceived by the listener as coming from a particular direction.
3.	Rapid fading	The sounds of human language do not persist over time; speech waveforms fade.
4.	Interchangeability	The speaker can both say and understand the same signal. We will discuss below examples of animal communication which do not have this property.
5.	Total feedback	The speaker can hear themselves speak and can alter their language performance.
6.	Reflexivity	People can talk about language; language has the ability to refer to itself.

7.	Specialization	The human mouth, tongue, throat, etc. have been specialized to be used for speech, instead of only being used for eating, as they are in many other animals.
8.	Semanticity	Specific signals can be matched with specific meanings. For example, in Spanish, the word *playa* refers to a pebbly or sandy shore.
9.	Arbitrariness	There is no connection between the form of a word and the thing that it refers to. For example, something as large as a sun can be referred to by a very short word.
10.	Discreteness	Speakers perceive each unit of speech as belonging to one category. For example, people who listen to a recording of a sound that falls physically somewhere between [t] and [d] perceive the sound as either a [t] or a [d], but not as a blend.
11.	Displacement	Language can refer to things which are not present in physical reality.
12.	Creativity	Speakers can create new sentences that others can understand.
13.	Traditional transmission	Although humans are born with an ability for language, they must be exposed to a language community in order to acquire their native language.
14.	Duality of patterning	The parts of a language can be recombined in a regular way to create new forms. For example, in English, the words *pat* and *tap* are different because of the order of the sounds.

2.2.2 Is Recursion the Key to Human Language?

Hauser, Chomsky, and Fitch (2002, p. 1571), in contrast to Hockett, propose that there is a single feature of human language that distinguishes it from all other animal communication systems: recursion. This relates back to our discussion in Chapter 1 of the "Infinite Complexity" of human language, where we observed that, "It seems that there is no limit to the complexity of the sentences that we may in principle utter or understand, since for every sentence that exists, there is a way to make that sentence more complex."

Recursion is the property of human language that makes it possible for every sentence to become a more complex sentence. We begin with the sentence in (2.1):

(2.1)

The boss is busy.

By placing this sentence inside a larger one, we can form a new and more complex sentence:

(2.2)

The assistant believes the boss is busy.

How is this possible? The sentence *The boss is busy* is still a sentence in (2.2), but now it has become part of a larger sentence that includes *The assistant believes* ... The key idea is that the sentence *The assistant believes* ... allows another sentence, *The boss is busy*, to be embedded within it. This is what linguists mean by recursion—we start with a structure and then add into that structure another structure of the same sort. Since this can continue on and on, there is no longest sentence of English—we could always have added more material to make each sentence larger.

Hauser, Chomsky, and Fitch (2002, p. 1571) claim that it is this property of human language which distinguishes it from all other forms of animal communication. As we discuss the varied forms of animal communication systems below, we return to this claim about the unique property of human language.

2.3 Properties of Animal Communication Systems

We have all wondered what animals are communicating to each other when they sing their melodious song, or they bark their vicious bark. Although it would be fascinating to find out what our cats say about us when chatting with their friends, it seems that progress in this area is in the distant future.

In this section, we discuss the communication systems of several animals which have developed a complex and advanced form of communication. We ask the question: Do these forms of communication share the key property of human language, recursion, that we discussed in Section 2.2? We explore this issue by taking a look at the general properties of animal communication and then discussing in detail the communication systems of the birds, the bees, and the cephalopods.

2.3.1 Forms of Animal Communication

Animals other than humans communicate in a wide variety of ways, including: chemical signals, visual signals, sounds, touch, smell, posture, and facial gesture. Of course, humans make use of many of these forms of communication as well.

2.3.1.1 Chemical Signals

Animals may use smell and taste in order to communicate with each other. For example, rabbits can release a fluid from glands in their chin that mark the ground within their territory. A rabbit may mark many acres of land in this way.

2.3.1.2 Visual Signals

Two types of visual communication among animals are badges, involving the color and shape of the animal, and displays, the things that animals do in order to communicate. An example of visual communication that is important in the study of animal communication is the parent herring gull's presentation of its bill. The herring gull has a bright yellow bill with a prominent red spot. A parent with food for its chicks stands over the chicks and taps its bill in front of them, and in response, the chicks peck at the spot in a begging motion. The adult bird then regurgitates food for the chicks.

The leading ethologist Niko Tinbergen proved that the contrast between the bright red and bright yellow colors of the herring gull's bill is important to the chicks' begging response. Gull chicks peck at everything that is brightly colored and contrastive—because of this, chicks sometimes die from swallowing pieces of brightly colored plastic or glass (Tinbergen, 1953).

2.3.1.3 Sounds

Animals use a variety of different sounds to communicate. For example, squirrels make a series of loud and distinctive calls when an intruder invades their territory. Dogs have a similar vocal response to outsiders approaching.

2.3.1.4 Touch

When a dog offers you its paw, they are communicating with you. A dog may be telling you that they want your attention or that they would like to be petted or played with. Animals use touch in many different ways. Some monkeys place their hand in the mouth of a monkey they are visiting and after a little while the other monkey reciprocates.

2.3.1.5 Smell

An example of a type of chemical communication involving smell is the defensive spray of the skunk. These animals have two glands which produce a mixture of sulfur-containing chemicals that has a distinctive and pungent smell which may be detected up to a mile away.

2.3.1.6 Posture

The posture of an animal may convey information about their emotional state and intention. For example, a dog with her tail up and stiff and a wrinkled nose with the corners of her mouth showing may be in an offensive threat posture.

2.3.1.7 Facial Gestures

Facial gestures are used by animals to express feelings and convey information. For example, when a dog wants to be left alone, he might yawn or lick his mouth. Mouth expressions that show aggression include the snarl, with the teeth exposed.

2.4 Animal Communication Systems

Dr. Stephen Anderson notes in his book *Dr. Dolittle's Delusion* (2006) that a human observer can know the temperature outside by listening to a cricket chirping. If we count the chirps during a period of 14 seconds and add 40, the result is the temperature in Fahrenheit. However, we cannot conclude from this that the cricket's behavior is intended to communicate the temperature to anyone—the rate of chirping depends on the insect's internal state alone, and happens automatically. Therefore, when we notice a predictable correlation between a particular animal behavior and something in the environment, we need to ask whether the animal intends to communicate information to another being by performing this behavior or whether the behavior is an automatic, internally determined behavior, and is thus quite different from human language.

In this section, we explore the properties of three animal communication systems which have been claimed to be significantly similar to human language: bee dance, birdsong, and cephalopod communication.

2.4.1 Bee Dances

Bees communicate with each other by using a series of complex dances. Certain bees in the hive are designated as forager bees: they go out in search of food sources for the hive. It had been noted many centuries ago that the dance of the bees is not random; certain information is conveyed by the dance. Aristotle described bees' behavior in his *Historia Animalium*: "Each bee on her return is followed by three or four companions ... how they do it has not yet been observed."

It was initially thought that the bee dance was used to attract the attention of other bees. However, in 1947, the Austrian scientist Karl von Frisch observed that, when a honey bee finds a feeding station, many other bees soon appear at the same station. This suggests that the first bee recruits other bees to the food. How might honey bees recruit help in collecting food? After careful investigation of the correlations between movements of bees inside the hive and the locations of feeding stations, von Frisch claimed that the runs and turns of the bee's movement correlates with the distance and direction of the food source from the hive (see von Frisch, 1927, 1967, 1973).

Western honey bees perform a dance on their return to the hive by utilizing a particular region in the comb, the dance floor. The dance floor is generally close to the entrance but may go further inside when it is cold or closer to the entrance when there is a lot of activity. Honeycombs are naturally vertical, and the dance is generally performed on a vertical plane. However, depending on the weather, the dance floor may move outside of the entrance to the hive and onto a horizontal direction.

The forager bee performs its dance in a circular pattern, occasionally crossing the circle in a zig-zag or waggle pattern. The distance of the food source is indicated by the type of dance performed by the forager bee: the round dance indicates a food source within the immediate vicinity of the hive, and the tail-wagging dance indicates that the distance is further. The forager bee also expresses the direction from the hive of the food source by its orientation with respect to the angle of the sun. The angle of the open side of the dance relative to the hive's vertical alignment indicates the direction of the flight toward the food source relative to the sun. Rather complex.

Bee dances communicate not only the location of the food source, but also the quality and quantity of the food. The level of intensity of the dancing expresses the quality of the food, and the vivacity of the dance shows the amount of food.

Linguists find this form of communication among bees interesting because it seems to show one of the defining properties of human language: its arbitrariness. There is no inherent connection between, for example, performing a dance in a tail-wagging pattern versus a round pattern and length of distance to a food source. Another significant property that bees' communication shows is displacement: the forager bee goes out to find the source of food and then returns to convey information that is not simultaneously present.

2.4.1.1 Experiments on Bee Communication

Karl von Frisch
Recall that in the 1940s the Austrian ethologist Karl von Frisch was the first to correlate the runs and turns of the bee dance to the distance and direction of the food source from the hive. His theory was disputed by other scientists and met with skepticism at the time. Only after many years was it definitively proven to be an accurate theoretical analysis. Von Frisch performed a series of experiments to validate his theory, and was awarded a Nobel Prize in 1973 for his discoveries.

Distinct Bee Dances
One of the most significant discoveries about the bee dance is that all of the known species of honey bees exhibit this behavior, but

details of its execution vary among the different species. For example, in dwarf honeybees, the dance is performed on the horizontal portion of the hive, whereas western honey bees perform their dance on a vertical plane, as noted above. Recall that the western honey bee relays the direction from the hive to the food source by its orientation with respect to the angle of the sun. In contrast, dwarf honey bees convey this information by moving directly toward the food source. Such species-specific behavior suggests that this form of communication does not depend on learning but is determined genetically.

In his experiments, von Frisch worked with Austrian bees, in which you will recall the distance of the food source is indicated by the type of dance performed by the forager bee: the round dance indicates a food source within the immediate vicinity of the hive, and the tail-wagging dance indicates that the distance is further. Interestingly, Italian bees communicate differently from Austrian bees in that they have an additional dance, the "sickle dance," in which the bees move in a crescent-shaped motion. This dance indicates that the food source is at an intermediate distance. On the surface, this distinction seems to be similar between the ones that exist among different human languages: they have the same basic structure, but their patterns are different.

However, as noted by Anderson (2006), we know in fact that these "dialects" of bee communication are not a matter of learning, but rather of biological necessity. When Italian bees are introduced into a hive of Austrian bees (after appropriate precautions are taken to prevent them from being killed), their dances are consistently interpreted by the Austrian bees in the wrong way—observers of the dance travel too far or too near from the hive in search of the food source. In addition, the bees never learn to change their dance or to understand the other bees' dance; it is determined by their genetics that they have the capacity to communicate in a single, unchangeable manner.

Further evidence for the genetically fixed view of the communication system of bees comes from the cross-breeding of Italian and Austrian bees. The cross-bred bees that bear a physical resemblance to their Italian parent perform the sickle dance to indicate intermediate distance, while the bees that bear a physical resemblance to their

Austrian parent perform the round dance to indicate intermediate distance; they do not perform the sickle dance at all. Researchers have thus concluded that the dance pattern associated with a bee is inherited from a certain parent along with other genetic traits. As noted by Anderson, this is different from what happens in human communities; when an Austrian and an Italian human have a child, the child learns whatever language or languages they are exposed to, regardless of whether they happen to look more like their mother or their father.

Although the communication system of bees is complex, it seems to differ significantly from human language in that bees are limited to communicating information about the location of a food source, whereas human language allows us to talk about anything that we would like to. In addition, our human biological endowment for language allows us to learn any human language, while the bees' form of communication seems to be fully determined by their genetic inheritance.

2.4.2 Birdsong

Birds communicate through two distinct methods: calls and song. Calls are used to communicate information such as warning of predators, to coordinate flocking and flight activity, and to express aggression or to accompany nesting or feeding behavior. For example, the cawing of crows is a typical call, used as a warning of possible danger. When other crows hear it, they fly higher up for protection.

The honking of geese in flight is an example of a call used to enable the flock to stay together. It is loud and easy to locate, thus serving its purpose well. In contrast, the call given by small birds when predators are present is different: it is typically thin and high-pitched, and therefore difficult to locate so that the position of the caller cannot be determined easily.

Birdsong is unlike calling in that it is musical and acoustically more complex. It is usually seasonal and only produced by male birds. The purpose of song is to announce and delimit the territory of the male and to attract a mate.

In some birds, song is a repetition of calls. In other birds, songs are comprised of complex patterns of pitches that form longer repeated units or themes. The song sparrow sings a loud song made up of repeating themes that usually begins with abrupt, well-spaced notes and finishes with a trill or buzz. Individual sparrows may add other units to the song with a different tempo.

Interestingly, researchers have discovered that there are call and song "dialects" among species: depending on the region of the country, a particular species of bird will have a distinct birdsong or call. This is a way in which bird communication seems similar to human communication.

2.4.2.1 Experiments on Birdsong

It is well known that human language development is subject to a sensitive period; if a person is not exposed to any human language until they are past what scientists call the "critical period"—probably from birth until around age 13—they will not develop a normal human language. (Later in the book we will discuss tragic instances of children raised in isolation who have been discovered beyond this critical period.)

In order to investigate the development of birdsong, Marler (1970) studied white-crowned sparrows. He found that if birds were raised in isolation from a few days after birth, they would not sing a well-developed white-crowned sparrow song when adult, but would sing a very crude song which had only some of the basic structure of the white-crowned sparrow song. When these isolated birds were exposed to a tape recording of a particular dialect of white-crowned sparrow song in the period of 10–50 days old, they would grow up to sing this full-blown song. If exposed to the same songs after the 50-day period, they would instead sing only the crude version of the song. Marler thus concluded that, like human language development, birdsong learning is subject to a sensitive period and cannot be acquired normally beyond this period.

Interestingly, different species of birds show distinct effects of nature and the environment on the learning of the song: the cuckoo learns the cuckoo song no matter what the environment, the bull-finch acquires any song from the environment, and the song sparrow shows some aspects of song developing the same way regardless of environment but other aspects dependent on the environment.

We have seen that bird calls and song are used to communicate information such as warning of predators, to coordinate flocking and flight activity, to announce and delimit the territory of the male, and to attract a mate. Although the communication system of birds is complex, we may ask if it shows the key property of human language—recursiveness.

Recall from our discussion earlier in the chapter that recursiveness in language is illustrated when a sentence becomes part of another sentence. This ability to "nest" structures allows us to continue building structure ad infinitum. Do bird calls and songs show this "nested" possibility? We have noted that bird songs may be comprised of complex patterns of pitches that form longer repeated units or themes. The key part of our description of this song is that it forms "longer repeated units or themes." This stringing along of units or themes may allow a longer song. However, does it illustrate recursiveness? If the bird song were recursive, then we would expect to find a pattern whereby a given unit or theme could be embedded within another unit or theme. However, it does not appear to be the case that bird song has this property, and therefore bird song, although complex and fascinating, seems not to have the property that has been argued to be the one unique human language property.

2.4.3 Vervet Alarm Calls

Another type of animal communication claimed by researchers to be highly complex is the alarm call system of vervet monkeys. These monkeys use different sounds to warn of different types of predator: they have distinct calls to warn of the sighting of a leopard, a snake, or an eagle. The calls are learned by monkeys with feedback from adult monkeys: when the young monkey makes the correct call, adult monkeys repeat the alarm. Punishment has also been observed. A young vervet sounded a "leopard" alarm to his mother, prompting her to run into hiding. However, there was no leopard, and the mother responded by "striking" her infant (Caro & Hauser, 1992; discussed in Morin, 2016).

The communication system of vervet monkeys is complex, and we may wonder if it has the crucial property of human languages— recursion. It seems that in the case of vervet monkeys, the referent of the call is necessarily immediate, and cannot be displaced; vervets cannot sound a call with the meaning "There was a leopard here a little while ago" or "There may be a snake coming along soon." In addition, vervets are limited to what they can express with their limited repertoire of calls; they cannot create a new call or combine existing calls through recursion in a way which will express something different from "There's a leopard!" or "There's a snake!" or "There's an eagle!"

2.4.4 Cephalopods

Cephalopods, a type of mollusk that include the octopus, squid, cuttlefish, and nautilus, possess a unique and complex communication system. The fishing industry name for this class is inkfish, referring to many cephalopods' ability to squirt ink.

Cephalopods are well known for their sophisticated use of color change for camouflage. Their advanced eyesight allows them to detect color and intensity of light especially well. In addition, they have special pigment cells which are linked to their nervous system. They are able to make use of these special cells to change color in order to match their environment.

Cephalopods also use color change and body posture to communicate with other cephalopods as well as with other species. In courtship rituals, males attempt to attract females by using color changes to show that they are suitable mates. During courtship, males will not only have to attempt to attract females, but also to fend off other males. Since their pigment cells are neurally controlled, the animal can produce a pattern on one side of its body in order to attract a female, while producing a completely different pattern on the other side which it directs at other males as a warning.

Cephalopods also use a high level of communication in fighting rituals. Squid's acts of aggression are mainly color displays and involve very little physical contact. These animals show various colors and body postures that increase with intensity until one fighter gives up.

While the use of color to communicate information in cephalopods is fascinating, does it appear to have the properties of a human language? If the cephalopods' communication system were recursive, then we would expect that these creatures would have the capacity to not only communicate two pieces of information at once to different audiences, but also have the general capacity to communicate messages embedded within each other. This, however, has not been attested in studies on cephalopods.

2.5 Conclusion

While animal communication systems allow a variety of distinct messages to be sent to others, compare this to human language. It is estimated that the average educated English-speaking person has a vocabulary of approximately 15,000 words. All speakers use these words to form sentences which are original and limitless.

On the other hand, the communication systems of non-human animals encode a fixed set of expressions—for example, how far away the pollen is, and in which direction (bees); danger approaching (monkey alarm calls). Human language, in contrast, is characterized by remarkable creativity, in the sense that humans can use their linguistic knowledge to create a vast array of different sentences, and regularly create novel sentences that they have never heard before. Therefore, linguists agree that the communication systems of other animals are not remotely as complex as human language.

You may wonder, however, if the reason that non-human animals have not developed as complex a communication system as humans is because they have not had the right environment—after all, babies speak a human language because they are exposed to one; they certainly do not grow up to speak a language that they have not been exposed to. Perhaps if the right kind of animal were raised in an environment in which human language were used all around them, they would be able to acquire human language. This is the topic that we turn to in the next chapter, which explores the work of scientists who have attempted to provide a normal human language environment for animals in order to see if they are then able to acquire a system as complex and creative as a human language.

Suggested Materials and Resources

Gondry (2013) presents in documentary form a wide-ranging and fascinating conversation with Noam Chomsky.

Arrival is a 2016 film about a linguistics professor who is called on to figure out how to talk to aliens (Villeneuve, 2016). The process of figuring out the alien language is a vital part of the plot.

A well-known and wide-ranging blog on linguistics can be found on the Language Log: http://languagelog.ldc.upenn.edu

For further discussion of the communicative abilities of non-human animals, see Anderson (2006) and Pinker (1994).

CHAPTER 3

Teaching Human Language to Apes

> If an animal had a capacity as biologically advantageous as
> language but somehow hadn't used it until now, it would be
> an evolutionary miracle, like finding an island of humans who
> could be taught to fly.
>
> Noam Chomsky (quoted in Atkinson, Bem, Smith, Renner, &
> Atkinson, 1993)

3.1 Introduction

In this chapter, we turn to the study of teaching human language to
other species. Scientists have reasoned that just because a species
does not have a communication system as complex as human
language in the wild does not necessarily prove that they are inca-
pable of using one. However, in attempting to teach human language
to other animals, we must avoid using features of language that are
physiologically difficult or impossible for the animal to manage. For
example, spoken human language is extremely difficult or impossible for most animals to produce because of the structure of their
vocal organs. Apes, for example, cannot produce a large proportion
of the vowels and would have difficulty with some of the consonants.
This may be due not only to the shapes of the vocal organs, but also
to the limitations of the motor centers in the brain that control
these organs. We might attempt, on the other hand, to teach apes
language that involves them using their hands (for example, signed
language or the manipulation of symbols).

We have seen that animal communication systems seem to lack unique features of human language. Therefore, researchers attempting to teach language to animals attempt to test for the existence of these features in the "language" use of their subjects.

3.2 Cautionary Tale—Hans the Horse

Clever Hans was a horse who became the toast of Berlin around the turn of the century. Hans could read, do math, and even solve problems of musical harmony. His owner, an elderly man named Wilhelm von Osten, had taught him the letters of the alphabet and corresponding numerals so that he could tap out replies. Hans captivated the public as well as the scientific communities (Bellows, 2008).

Skeptics of this clever horse investigated his surprising talents. Interestingly, they found that when Hans did not have a direct view of his owner, he was no longer able to perform his unusual feats. The psychologist Oskar Pfungst solved the puzzle when he noticed that the horse was picking up on the owner's breathing, posture, and facial expressions, which would, unknown to the owner, change ever so slightly as the "correct" tap was made with Hans's foot.

The term "Clever Hans Effect" is used today to describe the influence of a questioner's subtle and unintentional cues upon their subjects, in both humans and in animals. In order to avoid this effect, participants are not provided with knowledge about the goal of the experiment. For example, when dogs are being trained in drug-sniffing, none of the people involved know where the drugs are actually located; if they did, they could unconsciously tip off the dog with subtle cues and render the training useless.

3.3 Teaching Human Language to Apes

Why should we think that it might be possible to teach human language to non-human primates? Firstly, we are genetically very similar to these creatures: we share 98% of our genetic matter with chimpanzees and gorillas. All primates share a suite of physical features that allows them to be classified into the taxonomic order primate (from Latin, "prime, first rank"). Characteristic specializations of the limbs, eyes, nose, brain, teeth, and social behavior are common to all primates.

Non-human primates range in size from the Madame Berthe's mouse lemur, which weighs only 1.1 oz, to the mountain gorilla, weighing approximately 440 pounds. Some of the members of the class of primates are solitary animals, and some form part of complex social groups. Many are tree dwelling, and some are ground dwelling. There are quadrupeds and those that use bipedal locomotion. Except for humans, most primates live in tropical or subtropical regions of the Americas, Africa, and Asia. The hominoids include the baboon, which lives in central and northern Africa, the gibbon and the orangutan, which reside only in Southeast Asia, and the gorilla, chimpanzee, and humans.

3.3.1 Ape Communication in the Wild

As discussed in Chapter 2, in their natural environment, non-human primates are known to communicate with each other when warning about approaching danger—if a chimpanzee sees a snake, he may make a low, noisy rumble, which will signal for other chimps to move to safer ground. In this case, the chimpanzees' communication is entirely contained to an observable event, demonstrating a lack of displacement, the ability to refer to things which are not present in the environment.

3.3.1.1 Bonnet Macaque

The bonnet macaque is a South Asian monkey that displays an impressive system of 25 distinct vocalization patterns used for hostile encounters, foraging, greeting, and sexual contact. These patterns of vocalizations are claimed to occur in combinations, making them seem similar to human language. Recall, however, that the hallmark property of human language—its creativity—entails that new messages may be created by combining units of meaning in different ways. There appears to be no evidence that when distinct vocalizations are used, they are combined in novel ways to create new meanings; if this were possible, it would suggest that the communication system of the bonnet macaque is significantly similar to human language.

3.3.1.2 Goeldi's Monkey

Goeldi's monkey, found in South America, is claimed to have five distinct alarm signals, three of which are used for terrestrial predators, and two to signal the presence of birds. As was discussed in Chapter 2, vervet monkeys also show a regular connection between referent and vocalization, indicating that these monkeys have the cognitive capacity to associate categories of referents with vocalizations (Kirman, 2007).

3.3.1.3 Gibbons

Gibbons are unique among hominoids in showing a form of communication called duetting, in which calls are exchanged in a patterned manner between two gibbons (certain birds, bats, and antelopes also exhibit this behavior). Duetting seems to function to maintain spacing among territories (Guenole, 2013).

3.3.1.4 Orangutans

Unlike gibbons, which live in family groups, male orangutans are solitary animals: only mother and child orangutans pair together. Males use loud calls for territorial and spacing functions. The calls identify the rank of the male; high-ranking males approach calls made in the forest, whereas low-ranking males avoid areas where they hear the calls of high-ranking males.

3.3.1.5 Chimpanzees

Chimpanzees use as many as 16 distinct calls to communicate. Hooting signals location and is used to express greeting and excitement. A favorite food source elicits rough grunting. (See Chimpanzee Sanctuary Northwest, 2010 for examples of these distinct vocalizations.)

3.3.2 Experiments with Apes

Scientists would like to discover what capacities apes have that we may not be aware of. Given their genetic similarity, we might expect apes to be among the animals capable of communicating with human language. In this section, I describe experiments designed to discover if non-human primates are capable of learning language.

3.3.2.1 Gua

In the 1930s, the first psycholinguistic experiment designed to teach a human language to a non-human primate was designed by Luella Dorothy Agger and Winthrop Kellogg at the Yale Anthropoid Station in Florida. They raised Gua, an infant chimpanzee, alongside their baby son. At 16 months it was claimed that Gua understood about one hundred words, a number of verbal commands, some salutations, and a few instructions. Interestingly, Donald, the human "brother" of Gua, was found to have acquired a persistent habit of using chimp calls to ask for food, bringing an early close to the experiment. See Malone (2010) for an interesting look at the life of Gua.

3.3.2.2 Viki

In 1948, Viki, a baby chimpanzee, was trained to speak English over the course of 14 months by Catherine and Keith Hayes, who also worked with the Yale Anthropoid Station in Florida. Viki succeeded only in producing approximations of a couple of words such as *cup* and *papa*. Researchers soon concluded that the vocal anatomy of chimpanzees is inappropriate for producing human speech. The physiology of the epiglottis, an important flap of cartilage at the root of the tongue which closes when swallowing to block food from going down the windpipe, is constructed differently in humans than in chimpanzees. This distinction severely limits the range of human language sounds that chimpanzees can produce.

3.3.2.3 Washoe

Beatrice and Allen Gardner at the University of Nevada devised an experiment to teach human language to a chimpanzee which would overcome the problem of their inability to produce spoken language. They decided to teach her American Sign Language, since signed languages have all of the hallmark properties of spoken human language, and chimps are considered to be quite dexterous. The Gardners believed that the social context of language development in children was crucial, so they attempted to raise Washoe as a human child.

It was claimed that over a period of three years, starting in 1965, Washoe learned to produce 130 signs. Significantly, it was argued by the Gardners that Washoe was able to produce creative, new utterances. For example, she made the signs for *water* and *bird* when she saw a duck. She is also reported to have produced *baby in my cup* when her toy doll was placed in her cup. There has been much debate over whether these are instances of imitation on the part of Washoe or are actually creative behavior. If Washoe were able to create the utterance *baby in my cup* through applying the rule for forming a noun phrase (*my cup*) within another noun phrase (*baby in my cup*), then this would seem to be an example of a non-human primate exhibiting recursive linguistic behavior. (View wash001, 2009 for a description of how the Gardners attempted to teach signed language to Washoe).

What do you think of the linguistic capacity of Washoe—did she show human-like usage of linguistic structure, or was her communication system different in kind from a human language system?

3.3.2.4 Nim Chimpsky

In an attempt to prove that apes like Washoe were capable of using human language, in the early 1970s Herbert Terrace tried to teach American Sign Language to a chimp. He playfully named the animal Nim Chimpsky, after Noam Chomsky, a linguist renowned for his claim that only humans are capable of learning human language. After 44 months, Nim had learned approximately 125 signs. The longest recorded "sentence" of Nim's is *Give orange orange me give eat orange me eat orange give me eat orange give me me give give me you*. At first blush, it may seem impressive that a chimpanzee is able to create such a long utterance. However, this type of utterance is not typical of any documented human language and is not the type of utterance that children at any point in their development seem to use. You would probably be quite alarmed if your three-year-old niece came up to you and said, "Give orange orange me give eat orange me eat orange give me eat orange give me me give give me you."

On the other hand, Nim was reported to have produced utterances which are more typical of those of young children: *Hug me Nim, Me Nim eat, Me more eat.* Although Nim had communicated these rudimentary expressions, the chief researcher of the project Herbert Terrace argued that these were not in fact akin to the structures of human language, but were limited and non-creative. Terrace had begun the experiment to show that apes could learn human language, and he concluded that the experiment was a failure. This had strong repercussions on research with chimps—shortly after the experiment, there was a dearth of funding sources for this type of investigation. The film *Project Nim* (Marsh, 2011) provides a critical documentary of the work that was done with Nim Chimsky, within a broader discussion of the ethics of animal experimentation.

3.3.2.5 Lana

Critics of earlier chimpanzee experiments claimed that researchers were unconsciously cuing their subjects to produce signs (the "Clever Hans Effect"). In order to address this issue, Duane Rumbaugh and his team trained a chimp named Lana (an acronym for **Language Ana**logue) with a computer-controlled apparatus. Nine arbitrary symbols were manipulated by Lana to fulfill her needs for food, fresh air, grooming, and entertainment. Only the correct order of symbols in this invented language would elicit a reward for Lana. She successfully labeled and requested food and other items from the computer by using the symbols. See IowaPrimate.LearningSancturary (2010) for examples of Lana communicating.

3.3.2.6 Sarah

A young female chimp Sarah (at this point, you are probably starting to wonder, "Why are these chimps always female?") was taught by David Premack to manipulate arbitrarily shaped plastic symbols in order to receive rewards. She was claimed to be able to manipulate about 130 of these symbols. Utterances were formed by placing the tokens in a vertical line. Presented with the sentence *Brown color of chocolate* without any chocolate present, and later presented with *Take brown*, Sarah took a brown object. Utterances that Sarah created include *Sarah jam bread take* and *No Sarah honey cracker take*.

The experiment with Sarah proceeded in the following way: presenting the tokens for *Mary, give, banana, Sarah*, only this exact word order would elicit a reward; any other combination was not rewarded. Interestingly, when humans are taught to perform these tasks with plastic symbols, they perform as well as Sarah. However, humans have been argued to be utilizing general problem-solving skills and not linguistic analysis in this task. It is thus possible that Sarah's success in learning these tasks relies not on specifically linguistic training, but on the development of general problem-solving strategies.

3.4 Evaluating Ape Language Experiments

Experiments with teaching language to non-human primates are important in that they have established that these animals are capable of advanced symbol use and referential behavior. However, in addressing the question of whether a non-human primate can learn human language, recall that a crucial feature of all human languages is recursiveness, which provides a speaker with the ability to create and understand an unlimited number of novel sentences. It seems to be the case that it has not been shown that non-human primates have been able to acquire this capability. They have been able to learn signs as names for things or actions, but seem to be unable to go much beyond that.

In an influential paper in the journal *Science*, "Can an Ape Create a Sentence?" from 1979, Nim Chimpsky's trainer, Herbert Terrace, reluctantly concluded that the answer was "No." A chimp might learn to connect a hand sign with an item of food, Dr. Terrace argued, but this could be a matter of simple conditioning, like Pavlov's dogs learning to salivate at the sound of a bell. Most importantly, there was no evidence that the chimps had acquired a generative grammar—the ability to string words together into sentences of arbitrary length and complexity. Laura Pettito and Mark Seidenberg, two other researchers involved in the chimpanzee experiments, state, "We believe that ... there is no basis to conclude that signing apes acquired linguistic skills" (Terrace, Petitto, Sanders, & Bever, 1979, p. 891).

As stated by Noam Chomsky, "Human language appears to be a unique phenomenon, without significant analogue in the animal world ... There is no reason to suppose that the 'gaps' are bridgeable" (1972, p. 58). Not only is there no animal that is capable of achieving anything like human language, but also there is, at the other end of the scale, no human group that does not have a distinctively human language. As Comrie, Matthews, and Polinsky (2003) note, "No languageless community has ever been found."

The linguist Geoffrey Pullum succinctly states,

> I do not believe that there has ever been an example anywhere of a nonhuman expressing an opinion, or asking a question. Not ever. It would be wonderful if animals could say things about the world, as opposed to just signaling a direct emotional state or need. But they just don't.
>
> (Raffaele, 2006)

Suggested Materials and Resources

Project Nim, a 2011 British documentary film, focuses on attempts to teach Nim Chimpsky American Sign Language (Marsh, 2011).

View The Onion (2010) for a tongue-in-cheek report on the progress that primatologists have made recently demonstrating that "apes are capable of understanding their own mortality."

CHAPTER 4

Language Learning

The fact that all normal children acquire essentially comparable grammars of great complexity with remarkable rapidity suggests that human beings are somehow specially designed to do this, with data-handling or "hypothesis-formulating" ability of unknown character and complexity.

Noam Chomsky (1959)

4.1 Introduction

Every biologically normal child raised with other humans learns a human language. Regardless of their location, their living conditions, and their culture, there has never been discovered a group of people who do not have human language. It is for this reason that linguists consider human language to be essential to our nature.

There are claimed to be uncontacted groups of people throughout the world, groups who live in permanent isolation from the rest of the world. See Phillips (2016) for photos of an uncontacted group of Native Americans in Brazil. Isolated groups such as these Native Americans have been contacted throughout history, and all of them had a human language—a language which conformed to the principles and generalizations that linguists have posited to exist to be a hallmark of human language.

We therefore are faced with a very interesting question about our species: How do we all, regardless of our life circumstances and experiences, come to know language? Do children learn language from their parents and caregivers? Do children raised with different languages and in different cultures learn language differently? What role does the environment play in language learning?

Upon initial inspection, the language of a typical three-year-old child does not seem to be revealing of a highly abstract, complex, and rule-governed communication system.

(4.1) Star Wars according to a three-year-old (fistofblog, 2008)

> The sand people capture robots and drive and sell 'em ... at a garage sale ... kinda like a garage sale a-sept they're selling robots. And know who's gonna buy R2 and the shiny guy? The shiny guy always worries....

Although young children seem to lack considerable expressive ability that adults possess, consider that by the time children can walk they have spoken their first words and can comprehend about 50 words. When children are learning to run, they speak in full sentences and use language to control their environment (and their parents). The average three-year-old has the computational power and symbolic sophistication to do what our most advanced computers cannot do—to use human language to communicate with others, and to represent things in the past, the present, and the future. The average four-year-old has mastered the complex system of language and is able to converse with adults and peers.

4.2 Language Games

An example of the complexity and sophistication of child language comes from language games that children play. Read the following sentence. Do you understand it?

(4.2)

> Ethay idskay entway otay ethay orestay andway oughtbay omesay andiescay.

If you understand this sentence to mean the following, then you are probably familiar with Pig Latin:

(4.3)

The kids went to the store and bought some candies.

Pig Latin is a form of English which is used for secret communication. Speakers of Pig Latin may be fluent in this system of communicating (see kissmycats3093, 2009).

4.2.1 Rules of Pig Latin

The rules of Pig Latin that are unconsciously followed by its speakers are quite complex:

1. In words that begin with consonant sounds, the initial consonant or group of consonants ("consonant cluster") is moved to the end of the word, and *ay* is added, as in the following examples:

beast	→	*east-bay*
dough	→	*ough-day*
happy	→	*appy-hay*
string	→	*ing-stray*

2. In words that begin with vowel sounds or silent consonants, the syllable *way* is simply added to the end of the word. The syllable *ay* may be added, without the *w* in front.

another	→	*another-way* or *another-ay*
if	→	*if-way* or *if-ay*

3. In compound words (words made up of two words, such as *black-board*) or words with two distinct syllables, each component word or syllable may be manipulated separately, as in the following example:

birdhouse	→	*ird-bay-ouse-hay*

People who use Pig Latin have not been instructed overtly in the rules of this form of language—it seems unlikely that children understand and express concepts such as consonant clusters and compound words with distinct syllables. Unless an adult studies linguistics, she is unlikely to ponder these phenomena. Rather, it seems that as humans we have the capacity to just "pick up" language forms that are presented to us and unconsciously extract from language data generalizations and rules that allow us to create new forms.

We are left with the question: Just how do children at such a young age pick up the abstract rules of language without being taught them? There are several possible explanations: perhaps parents (or care-takers) teach language to their children; or perhaps kids automatically grow a language just by being in a language environment. We consider several hypotheses of language acquisition in this chapter.

4.3 Parental Input

It is commonly thought that parents teach their children language, and linguists have investigated this claim to determine if parental behavior with children is crucial to language development. There are several ways in which it is possible that parents might teach their children language: by overt instruction, using correction and reward, or by covert instruction, whereby the parent behaves in a way which is conducive to language learning, although they might not be aware of it.

4.3.1 Overt Teaching

Many parents believe that they teach their children to speak, and they thus consider it important to correct their children when they say something that does not sound like adult English. For example, the child, pointing at a toy, says, "wan tha," and the parent says, "Say, 'I WANT THAT'."

Linguists have analyzed large stretches of interaction between children and their parents to try to determine if there is a correlation between parents' corrections and children's progress in learning language. Brown and Hanlon (1970) conducted a major study of child–parent interactions and made several interesting conclusions.

Brown and Hanlon note that ungrammatical sentences are actually rarely corrected by parents. A typical example of a child–parent interaction where the child is not corrected is the following:

(4.4)

Child: Doggie bited daddy.
Mother: Yes, that's right.

They observe that, in general, parents correct what children say if their statement is untrue, rather than if it is grammatically correct. The following examples illustrate this:

(4.5)

Joey (child):   Joey not hit Laurie.
Mother: Now Joey, that's not true.

Child: Momma isn't a boy, he a girl.
Mother: That's right.

Furthermore, Brown and Hanlon note that when parents **do** try to teach their children, they are generally ignored. The following is a classic interaction recorded by David McNeill that illustrates this (McNeill, 1966, p. 69):

(4.6)

Child: Nobody don't like me.
Father: No, say, "Nobody likes me."
Child: Nobody don't like me.
Father: No, you say, "Nobody likes me."
Child: Nobody don't like me.
Father: No, listen, say, "Nobody likes me."
Child: Nobody don't like me.
Father: No, say, "Nobody likes me."
Child: Nobody don't like me.
Father: No, you have to say, "Nobody likes me."
Child: Nobody don't like me.
Father: No, I said, say, "Nobody likes me."
Child: Nobody don't like me.
Father (exasperated):   No, now listen carefully; say, "Nobody ... likes ... me."
Child (big smile):   Oh!!!! Nobody don't **likes** me!!

When children encounter their native language, they are exposed to a continuous stream of sounds—but how do they segment this speech stream into the words of their language? When we listen to a language that we do not know, we realize that this is no easy task. There are no pauses or indicators that one word has ended and another has begun. Thus, a key question in language acquisition is how children are able to pick out the individual words from what sounds like a continuous stream of speech.

4.3.2 Indirect Teaching

Several researchers have proposed that, although children may not rely on overt corrections by parents, they may perhaps depend on subtle, unconscious behaviors of parents in order to learn their language. For example, perhaps parents respond differently to grammatical versus ungrammatical utterances from their children. Brown and Hanlon investigated this claim, and they noted an instance in which the mother responded distinctly to her child's ungrammatical utterance:

(4.7)

Child:	What time it is?
Mother:	Uh, huh, it tells what time it is.

The child here seems to be asking for the time, but the mother responds to the question as if it were a statement: *It tells what time it is*. Importantly, this is the only example that Brown and Hanlon found in their data of distinct responses to children's ungrammatical utterances. The typical pattern that they found is illustrated in (4.8):

(4.8)

Adult:	I don't think you write with pencil on that, Adam.
Adam:	What you write with?
Adult:	You write with some crayons.
Adam:	Why d(o) you carry it by de handle?

The ungrammatical sentence *What you write with?* should be *What do you write with?* However, the parent does not respond to this sentence differently than if it were produced correctly, continuing on with the conversation to say, *You write with some crayons.* It thus seems that parents neither regularly correct their children's ungrammatical utterances nor respond differently to them than to grammatical utterances. This supports the claim that parental input does not play an important role in the language acquisition process.

4.3.2.1 Motherese

It is common to hear parents speaking to their children in what linguists call "Motherese." This "babytalk" consists of reduplicated syllables, such as *baba* for blanket and diminutive endings, such as *horsey* for horse. Parents often use the third person instead of first and second person when speaking with children, as in *Mummy loves little Joey* instead of *I love you.* Snow and Newport have reported that the sound patterns of motherese include higher overall pitch, wider and smoother pitch excursions in intonation contours, slower tempo, and longer pauses between utterances (Snow, 1972; Newport, 1975; Snow & Ferguson, 1977).

Interestingly, the sentence structures directed toward children also seem to differ from those directed toward adults: linguists have noted that child-directed speech has twelve times as many questions, nine times as many commands, and one-third as many statements as adult-directed speech. Could this aid the child in learning her language?

4.3.2.2 Questions about Motherese

There is wide variation in the language practice of parents with their children across the world. However, it does not seem to be the case that children differ in the way in which they learn language according to the type of linguistic environment in which they grow—researchers have argued that the sequence and processes of acquisition are identical across children reared in very different environments. (Ochs, 1982; Ratner & Pye, 1984; Schieffelin & Ochs, 1987; Ingram, 1989; Phillips, 1994; Schieffelin, 1994; Shneidman & Goldin-Meadow, 2012; Levine & Munsch, 2013). Also note that the end product of first-language acquisition is 100% perfect attainment—the children of parents who spend much of their time making enough money to buy food do not attain a level of language knowledge which is distinct in any manner from the children of parents who spend much of their time chatting with their babies.

In addition to this consideration, recall that linguists have noted that child-directed speech has far more questions and commands and far fewer statements than adult-directed speech. Steven Pinker notes that this in fact makes child-directed speech more structurally complex than adult-directed speech. For example, consider the way in which we form questions in English. In order to turn this sentence:

(4.9)

Rich will leave the room.

into a yes-no question, we move the words around, to form:

(4.10)

Will Rich leave the room?

English has a rule of question formation which can thus be formulated as follows:

(4.11) English Question Formation Rule (Version 1)

In order to form a question from a statement, switch the position of the first two words in the sentence.

However, we would like our rule to correctly generate the form of all possible English questions. Note that the English Question Formation Rule (Version 1) will not explain how the following sentence turns into a question:

(4.12)

The boy will leave the room.

If we apply the English Question Formation Rule (Version 1) to this sentence, we get (4.13):

(4.13)

   *Boy the will leave the room?

We have switched the position of the first two words in the sentence. Recall that the star (*) that occurs before this sentence indicates that it is not a sentence that a speaker of English would say (unless they were sitting in a linguistics class trying to come up with a counter-example to the English Question Formation Rule (Version 1)). Therefore, we need to update our English Question Formation Rule in order to explain why it works the way that it does to form the natural:

(4.14)

   Will the boy leave the room?

We could update the rule as follows:

(4.15) English Question Formation Rule (Version 2)

> In order to form a question from a statement, switch the position of the verb to the front of the sentence.

However, note that this rule incorrectly predicts that the sentence in (4.12) can turn into a question by saying the following:

(4.16)

   *Leave the boy will the room?

Example (4.16) follows the rule in (4.15), since we have moved the verb *leave* to the front of the sentence, but this is not how a speaker of English would produce this sentence (although if someone came up to you on the street and said, "Left the boy will the room?", you would probably understand what she meant, but you would be wondering to yourself, "Why the heck did she say it that way?").

It seems that we need to distinguish between main verbs, such as *leave*, and auxiliary verbs, such as *will*. We can restate the English Question Formation Rule as in (4.17):

(4.17) English Question Formation Rule (Version 3)

In order to form a question from a statement, switch the position
of the auxiliary verb to the front of the sentence.

Note that this statement of the rule predicts that the sentence in
(4.18) should be able to be turned into a question by making it into
(4.19)

(4.18)

The boy should have left the room?

(4.19)

*Have the boy should left the room?

Since both *should* and *have* are auxiliary verbs, moving *have* to the
front is predicted to be correct. However, we know that we can only
form the question as follows:

(4.20)

Should the boy have left the room?

We could then change again our English Question Formation Rule to
be:

(4.21) English Question Formation Rule (Version 4)

In order to form a question from a statement, switch the position
of the first auxiliary verb to the front of the sentence.

However, note that this rule does not make the correct prediction for
the following sentence, that does not have an auxiliary verb:

(4.22)

The boy left the room.

It is not possible to apply English Question Formation Rule
(Version 4) to the sentence in (4.22), since there is no auxiliary in the
sentence. In fact, the way in which we form the question counterpart
to (4.22) is as follows:

(4.23)

Did the boy leave the room?

So, it appears that if there is no auxiliary verb in the sentence, we create an auxiliary verb with *do* and move that verb to the front of the sentence. Therefore, we may reformulate the English Question Formation Rule as in (4.24):

(4.24) English Question Formation Rule (Version 5)

> In order to form a question from a statement, switch the position of the first auxiliary verb to the front of the sentence. If the sentence does not contain an auxiliary verb, insert the auxiliary verb *do* and move the tense of the verb to the auxiliary *do*.

Let us step back from our discussion of the correct formulation of the English Question Formation Rule. Now imagine sitting a three-year-old child down to work through with them the precise formulation of this rule (Version 644). It is not going to happen. We can safely conclude that there is no overt teaching involved in the acquisition of this rule of English.

Perhaps the overabundance of these structures is helpful to children learning language. But as linguists have noted (Pinker, 1994), how could it be that having a preponderance of questions in the language directed to children could possibly help the children acquire English; given that the rule underlying these sentences is extremely complex and abstract, these utterances would seem to be the least optimal for teaching young learners the basics of their language. Imagine if you were learning a new language and the sentences that you had access to were questions where items had been moved around; would this help you to learn the regular structure of the language?

A second objection to the claim that motherese assists children in learning language comes from researchers who have noted that not all cultures use motherese. While researchers have confirmed that the characteristics of motherese are found in languages as typologically varied as Chinese (Greiser & Kuhl, 1988), Japanese (Masataka, 1992), and various European languages (Fernald et al., 1989), there are cultures which do not utilize motherese. For example, research on language development among the Quiché in Guatemala has shown that parents ignore the infant until it produces "recognizable adult-like language" (Ingram, 1998).

According to Clifford Pye (1983), "Quiché parents spend their time working, not entertaining their children. I did not observe (nor could I elicit) any traditional games or songs which parents engaged in with their young children" (Ingram, 1989). Nevertheless, children raised in these cultures successfully learn their language.

4.4 The Role of Imitation and Repetition

According to the behaviorist view of human development, children learn language by imitating and repeating what they hear. This approach seems to be intuitive, since we know that children exposed to Japanese learn Japanese and children exposed to Swahili learn Swahili. B. F. Skinner developed this approach to language acquisition in his 1957 book *Verbal Behavior*. Far better known than the book itself, however, is a scathing review that the young linguist Noam Chomsky wrote (Chomsky, 1967), in which he argued that the behaviorist paradigm was fatally flawed. This review has been hailed as the most influential document in the history of psychology. It signaled the beginning of the Cognitive Revolution in linguistics. In his review of Skinner's book, Chomsky noted that, although children repeat words and phrases heard in the environment, imitation alone cannot possibly account for all of language acquisition. This is because children say things that they could not have heard. The capacity for children to say new things can be funny, as when a mom and her three-year-old have a conversation and the mom says, *I love you*, to which the child responds, *I only love you when you give me cookies*. Presumably the child has not heard this sentence before.

This creative capacity of children is also linguistically significant, as when children produce new words such as *underbrella* (umbrella), *tree-knocker* (woodpecker), and *flutterby* (butterfly). Children make grammatical mistakes that they could not have been exposed to. For example, they say things such as:

(4.25)

   a.   Cookies are gooder than bread.
   b.   Bill taked the toy.
   c.   We goed to the store.
   d.   Don't giggle me.

It is unlikely that someone in the child's environment is saying, *We goed to the store*. In situations in which the input to the child is irregular, the child creates from this irregular input a systematic and regular language structure, as in examples of creolization or in the creation of Nicaraguan Sign Language—see Degraff (2005) for discussion of Haitian Creole and Kegl (2002) and Senghas, Senghas, and Pyers (2005) for relevant discussion of the emergence of signed language in Nicaragua.

As parents know, these errors are not random "mistakes"; every child learning English passes through a stage where they produce such errors. They are examples of overgeneralization—the application of a rule that the child is learning to data that are exceptions to the rule.

Generally, we form the past tense of verbs in English by adding the suffix -*ed* to the verb, as in *wanted, lasted*, etc. However, there are many exceptions to this rule: *eat–ate, see–saw, hit–hit, read–read*. Since children initially analyze words as indivisible units, they originally produce irregular forms like *ate*; they will say things like *I eat apples every day* and *Yesterday I ate apples*. They then start to learn the regular rule of past tense formation in English, and apply this generalization initially across the board, and hence produce sentences like *Yesterday I eated apples*. This is usually the point at which a parent starts to freak out because the child had been producing the adult-like irregular form and then seems to "regress" to producing a non-adult-like form. What appears distressing to parents is in fact evidence that children are acquiring a regular, rule-based system.

So, it seems that children do not simply imitate the language that they hear around them. They deduce rules from it, which they can then use to produce sentences that they have never heard before. They do not learn a repertoire of phrases and sayings, as behaviorism claimed, but a grammar that generates an infinite number of new sentences. In sum, as R. L. Trask has stated it, "One of the most profound and indisputable achievements of linguistics in recent years has been the demonstration that this imitation and reinforcement model is totally, hopelessly, grotesquely wrong" (Trask, 1999, p. 168).

4.5 Universals in Language Acquisition

The claim that language acquisition follows a predetermined, biologically specified path in humans is supported by the observation that there are many logically possible errors that children do not seem to make. For example, recall from our discussion of language learning in non-human primates that we would be surprised if we heard our three-year-old niece say something like *Give orange orange me give eat orange me eat orange give me eat orange give me me give give me you* (which is what Nim Chimpsky produced). Although that is a form of communication that would convey the meaning intended, it seems that there is no grammatical system that a child entertains that will generate such utterances.

Chomsky claims that the reason that language acquisition proceeds in a systematic fashion is that human beings are structured in such a way that they consider only certain hypotheses about the language they develop. The process of language learning is guided by Universal Grammar, the aspect of language which is common to all human languages and is pre-wired in humans (see Klima & Bellugi, 1966 for discussion). An example of a principle of Universal Grammar is the Principle of Structure Dependency. Structure Dependency is stated as in (4.26):

(4.26) Principle of Structure Dependency (Chomsky, 1971, p. 30)

All formal operations in the grammar of human language are dependent on the abstract structure of the sentence.

In order to understand how this principle functions, recall from the discussion above that in devising a rule that would describe the process of Question Formation in English, we, on the basis of examples such as (4.27), formulated the rule as in (4.28):

(4.27)

    a.   Rich will leave the room.

    b.   Will Rich leave the room?

(4.28) English Question Formation Rule (Version 1)

    In order to form a question from a statement, switch the position
    of the first two words in the sentence.

Recall from our discussion, however, that the English Question Formation Rule (Version 1) does not account for how the following sentence turns into a question:

(4.29)

    The boy will leave the room.

If we apply the English Question Formation Rule (Version 1) to this sentence, we get (4.30):

(4.30)

    *Boy the will leave the room?

In (4.30), we have switched the position of the first two words in the sentence. Notice that the process of question formation as stated in (4.28) violates the Principle of Structure Dependency, since it is stated on the basis of the linear order of the words in the sentence as opposed to the grammatical structure of the sentence.

Recall that there is an overabundance of questions such as *Will Peter leave the room?* in the language directed to children. Therefore, it is plausible that children would entertain the hypothesis that question formation in English is stated as a process of switching the first two words of the sentence. If this were the case, we would expect children to go through a stage at which they would produce sentences such as the unacceptable *Boy the will leave the room?*

Linguists have investigated whether this prediction is borne out and have concluded that children do not in fact spontaneously produce sentences such as (4.30) and, in experimental conditions, do not produce such sentences when they are prompted to (Crain & Nakayama, 1987).

We can understand this if children are genetically endowed with Universal Grammar, which limits the hypotheses children consider as they acquire language. Children do not hypothesize a process such as (4.22), because humans are not able to hypothesize such a process.

4.6 Stages of Acquisition

While there is variation in the age at which children acquire certain language structures, the order in which these structures is acquired is universal. It is important to keep in mind that language development is typically characterized by gradual acquisition of particular abilities: thus, mastery of English verb endings emerge over a period of a year or more, starting from a stage where verb endings are always left out and ending in a stage where they are used as in the adult grammar.

At birth, the infant vocal tract is more similar to an ape's than an adult human's. The pharynx of an adult human is significantly longer than that of human babies and apes. As a result of this, the adult tongue can move in a way that creates an enclosed space of different sizes, allowing us to produce distinct speech sounds. On the other hand, with a shorter pharynx, the vocal repertoire of apes and babies is decidedly fixed. (Several researchers have argued that monkeys' vocal tracts are "speech-ready", and thus the only reason that these animals do not have speech is neural [Fitch, de Boer, Mathur, & Ghanzafar, 2016]. However, see Lieberman [2017] for arguments against this view.)

We will see interesting evidence in Chapter 5 that, even while children cannot produce very sophisticated sounds or words, they nonetheless show evidence of having acquired word meanings and differences between different sounds.

4.6.1 Speech is Special

Newborns can distinguish speech from non-speech, and can also distinguish among speech sounds (e.g. [t] vs. [d] or [t] vs. [k]). Within a couple of months of birth, infants can distinguish speech in their native language from speech in other languages.

Children pass through regular stages in the production of their language—in this section, we look at children's development by examining what children say. However, we will see in Chapter 5 that, in terms of what they know, children seem to be way ahead of what they can say.

4.6.1.1 Vocalization

In the first two months of life, babies' expressions are usually crying and fussing, along with sounds produced in conjunction with swallowing, such as coughing, sucking, and burping. There are some sounds produced with the back of the roof of the mouth lowered and a closed or nearly closed mouth, giving the impression of a vowel sound produced through the nose.

4.6.1.2 Cooing

From about two to four months, infants begin vocalizing with grunts and sighs, and they later start to make typical cooing sounds. These sounds are usually brief and isolated and, as the baby grows, they appear in a series and are connected. Most children start making laughing sounds at about four to five months.

4.6.1.3 Vocal Play

In the period from four to seven months, infants engage in "vocal play," making pleasurable coos and gurgles. At this time, babies begin to pay attention to speech and may use intonation, seeming to be trying to talk with people and things around them.

4.6.1.4 Babbling

At about seven months, babies begin to extend vowel sounds, such as *maaaaaaa, uuuuuuuuuum*. This develops into more advanced babbling in which the baby produces sequences of consonant and vowel sounds such as *ma ma ma ma ma* or *ba ba ba ba*. Eventually children will mix these patterns together and produce sounds such as *gamama* and *bamaga*, and *gagameeeee*. These sounds are produced with caregivers, but also when babies are alone.

4.6.1.5 One-Word Stage

At ten to twelve months, babies begin to produce identifiable words. Most commonly, babies name items around them and may over-extend or underextend the meaning of a word—for example, referring to all animals as *dog*, or using the word *cat* only with a particular toy cat.

In their second year, children show a rapid increase in their vocabulary. Production diaries (recordings of children's early speech) indicate that children acquire approximately one to three new words per week. From the third year onwards, children show an accelerated growth of new words: children learn about ten new words each day during their pre-school and elementary school years.

4.6.1.6 Two-Word Stage

During the second year, word combinations begin to appear. At a year and a half, many parents report that their child is combining words. Most children are combining words by the age of two years, although they also engage in one-word utterances and babbling.

Examples of typical two-word utterances are: *mommy* and *hat* combined as *mommy hat*; *shirt* and *wet* combined as *shirt wet*.

(4.31)

    a.   Baba fall.
    b.   Mummy go.
    c.   See tv.

These combinations tend to occur in the order that is appropriate for the language being learned. For example, English-speaking children say, *See tv*, whereas a Japanese child says the following, since in adult Japanese, the verb comes after the object:

(4.32)

> *Ringo-o*   *tabe-ru*
> Apple-ACC   eat-NONPAST
> "Eat apple."

Typically absent at this stage of development are words that carry grammatical information, such as verbal endings, auxiliary verbs such as *will*, articles such as *the*, etc.

4.6.1.7 Telegraphic Stage

Children in the early multi-word stage typically leave out grammatical words, even when they are asked to repeat sentences that contain these words.

(4.33)

> Mother: I can see a cow.
> Child: See cow.   (child at 25 months)

(4.34)

> Mother: The doggy will bite.
> Child: Doggy bite.   (child at 28 months)

(4.35)

> Mother: Kathryn doesn't like celery.
> Child: Kathryn no like celery.   (child at 22 months)

(4.36)

> Mother: The baby doll rides a truck.
> Child: Baby doll ride truck.   (child at 22 months)

(4.37)

> Mother: The pig says oink.
> Child: Pig say oink.   (child at 25 months)

Typical examples of other multi-word utterances are:

(4.38)

Child: Want lady get chocolate.   (child at 23 months)

(4.39)

Child: Car going?   (with meaning: (child at 21 months)
                        "Where is the car
                        going?")

The pattern of leaving out most grammatical endings is called "telegraphic speech."

4.6.1.8 Multi-word Stage

Children do not typically use grammatical forms until about 24 months. Grammatical forms are words and parts of words that play a role in the sentence, for example: verb endings (*want-ed* and *want-s*), distinct pronouns (*he* versus *him*), complementizers (*I said that Mary is nice*), and articles (*the, a*). Note that initially telegraphic utterances are used at the same time as their adult version:

(4.40)

She's gone. Her gone school.   (child at 24 months)

(4.41)

He's kicking a beach ball. Her climbing up   (child at 24 months)
the ladder there.

(4.42)

I teasing Mummy. I'm teasing Mummy.   (child at 24 months)

(4.43)

I having this. I'm having 'nana.   (child at 27 months)

(4.44)

I'm having this little one. Me'll have that.   (child at 30 months)

(4.45)

Mummy haven't finished yet, has she?   (child at 36 months)

From the age of 12 months to 18 months, children use longer sentences, and grammatical elements are more frequently included and used in an adult-like fashion.

4.7 Acquisition of Grammatical Markers

Brown (1973, p. 308) noted that there is a consistent order that children follow in their learning of grammatical markers. Recall that examples of grammatical markers are verb endings, distinct pronouns, complementizers, and articles. Brown's table is shown below:

Order of acquisition of grammatical markers (Brown, 1973, p. 308)

1.	present progressive	*sing<u>ing</u>*
2/3.	prepositions	<u>*in*</u>, <u>*on*</u>
4.	plural	*cat<u>s</u>*
5.	irregular past tense	<u>*went*</u>, <u>*hit*</u>
6.	possessive	*Mary'<u>s</u> book*
7.	copula verb, not contracted	*Mary <u>is</u> tall.*
8.	articles	<u>*the*</u> *bike*
9.	regular past tense	*want<u>ed</u>, lov<u>ed</u>*
10.	3rd person present, regular	*Joe brush<u>es</u> his teeth.*
11.	3rd person present, irregular	*John <u>does</u> homework.*
12.	auxiliary, not contracted	*Mary <u>is</u> running.*
13.	copula, contracted	*John'<u>s</u> in the room.*
14.	auxiliary, contracted	*Mary'<u>s</u> running.*

Perhaps, you may wonder, do children learn in this order only because certain structures are more frequent in the language environment? In fact, Brown (1973, p. 356) wondered the same thing: "We wanted to be able to test the hypothesis that the frequencies with which particular morphemes are modeled for a child by his parents affects the order in which the child acquires those morphemes." Brown analyzed the speech of the parents of the children he was recording as they were talking with their children, recording only the speech directed to the child. Although Brown found that there was a pattern across the parents in terms of the frequency with which they used the different morphemes, he concludes that "no relation has been demonstrated to exist between parental frequencies and child's order of acquisition" (1973, p. 362).

It therefore seems that there is a significant generalization about the order of acquisition of the major grammatical markers of English, across different children. While researchers have proposed different explanations of this generalization, all agree that this claim is significant and robust.

4.8 The Acquisition of Negation

As has been noted since the earliest studies on language acquisition, in negating sentences children pass through three stages in a regular sequence (Bellugi, 1967):

(4.46)

a.	*No* at the front of the sentence:	*No I want juice.*
b.	*No* precedes the verb:	*I no want juice.*
c.	Correct placement of negation:	*I don't want juice.*

One approach to explaining generalizations about the linguistic behavior of young children is to understand acquisition as the process of passing from one adult-like grammar to another. In other words, children begin the process of acquisition assuming (unconsciously) that the language that they are learning will choose between different possible structures. This is known as the Parameter Setting Approach to language learning.

This approach allows us to understand why all children learning English produce negative sentences that they have never heard; given that there are human languages in which negation appears before the verb, researchers have suggested that perhaps all children pass through a stage with the Parameter of Negation set to the structure of pre-verbal position.

Consider negation in Spanish. The counterpart to the English sentence in (4.47a) is (4.47b):

(4.47)

a.   John doesn't study literature.

b.   Juan no estudia literatura.

In Spanish, and many other languages, the negative word is placed before the main verb in general. English requires the use of an auxiliary verb to express negation, and if there is no auxiliary verb in the sentence, the verb *do* is used. (Recall that this is similar to the pattern that we saw above for forming questions in English—if there is an auxiliary verb, it moves to the front of the sentence, but if there is no auxiliary verb, *do* is added and is used as an auxiliary.)

The child learning English then passes onto a stage where negation is correctly realized only with an auxiliary verb, whereas the child learning Spanish does not need to revise their hypothesis about negation. Note that this approach predicts that Spanish-speaking children do not pass through a stage where they treat negation as it is in English—in other words, Spanish-speaking children are predicted to not pass through a stage where they would require an auxiliary verb present in every negative sentence. As discussed by Déprez and Pierce (1993), this seems to be correct.

4.9 Production versus Perception

Notice that the discussion of the acquisition of language by children has thus far been framed in terms of what it is that children say. However, there is good reason to think that as children progress through the acquisition process, they have the capacity to understand much more than they say.

Diary studies are a commonly used method in language acquisition research, where a caregiver keeps a regular record of what the child says. Benedict (1979) asked caregivers to keep a diary indicating not only what words children produced, but what words they gave evidence of understanding. The results indicate that at the time when children were producing 10 words, they were estimated to understand 60 words. There was an average gap of five months between the time when a child understood 50 words and the time when she produced 50 words.

Intriguingly, several studies have shown that children who regularly omit grammatical elements in their speech nevertheless expect these elements in the speech of adults:

(4.48)

Dad:	Where's mommy?
Child:	Mommy goed to the store.
Dad:	Mommy goed to the store?
Child:	NO! Daddy, I say it that way, not you!

This discrepancy between what children understand and what they are able to produce introduces interesting complexities to the systematic exploration of children's language development, a topic that we turn to in Chapter 5.

4.10 Conclusion

In this chapter, we have seen that biologically normal children who are raised in a language community acquire their language in a predictable and principled fashion. Although the early speech of children may appear chaotic, when we examine in detail what children say and when they say it, all children pass through the same stages of language learning.

We have seen, however, that children seem to be able to understand more than they produce. In the following chapter, we turn to a discussion of this issue and we investigate in detail how researchers in language acquisition set up experiments that can be performed on young children who do not yet have the capacity to produce certain information but nonetheless seem to have knowledge of it.

Suggested Materials and Resources

See Searchinger (1995) for three films about the structure of human language, the acquisition of language, and the evolution of language.

CHAPTER 5

Experiments in Language Acquisition

5.1 Introduction

The previous chapter outlined the universal processes of language learning that all children progress through as they acquire their native language. This discussion was based on children's language production. However, it appears that children have linguistic knowledge before they produce it. Researchers have thus developed a specialized methodology for doing experiments with children in order to discover what their unconscious knowledge of language is. In this chapter, we explore these methodologies.

Consider now how the language acquisition process might be different for non-native speakers of a language. At first glance, it may seem more straightforward to investigate language acquisition with adults than with infants, since we will not have to resort to complex experiments in order to find out what adults know about their language—unlike children, who may not yet be able to speak, adults can tell us what they know and what they do not know about their language. Or can they? In fact, adult native speakers of a language do not have conscious knowledge of the properties of their language. In order to see this, ask three English speakers why we cannot say the negative form of the sentence *John saw Mary* by saying *John not saw Mary*. Recall from Chapter 2 that, although in many languages it is possible to form a negative sentence in this way, we need to follow a complex rule for forming negative sentences in English in which we add a verb *did* and attach *n't* to the end of this verb, as in *John didn't see Mary.* Although everyone who knows English recognizes that this is the way we form a negative sentence, the explanation for why it is that we form this type of sentence in this way is a mystery to all except those who have delved into the scientific study of language. We will see in our discussion of second language acquisition that finding out what adults know about their second language is not a straight-forward process and requires that we develop methods for accessing this unconscious knowledge.

5.2 Infants Distinguish All Speech Sounds

Researchers have shown that infants begin their language learning experience with the capacity to distinguish among all speech sounds (Werker & Tees, 1984). Since each language makes use of only some of the possible speech sounds, children eventually lose their ability to distinguish speech sounds which are not present in their language. Anyone who has studied a foreign language as an adult understands how difficult it is to learn to distinguish sounds not present in your native language; however, when you were six months old, you had that capacity.

Some speech sounds exist in some languages, but not others. For example, English has two consonant sounds produced with the tongue tip located between the teeth:

(5.1)

this

(5.2)

think
(Notice that although these sounds are written the same, with "th," they are two different sounds.)

These interdental ("between the teeth") sounds are rare in the languages of the world. It is therefore not surprising that people learning English as a non-native language typically experience significant difficulty in mastering these sounds.

There is another way in which languages may differ with respect to their sound systems. For example, English has two types of vowels: oral and nasal. Oral vowels are produced when the speech sound comes out of the mouth, and nasal vowels are produced when the speech sound comes out of the nose. There is a generalization about where these different types of vowels appear in English: all vowels in English are oral, unless they are followed by a nasal consonant, in which case they become nasal (Berger, 2008). In order to see this, compare the pronunciation of the /a/ sound in the following two words:

(5.3)

   cat

(5.4)

   can

The vowel sound is the same, except that when it is pronounced before a nasal sound such as /n/, as in (5.4), the vowel sound itself is nasal. You can see this by holding your nose as you produce these two words—when we produce *cat*, the word sounds the same whether we are holding our nose or not. However, when we produce the word *can*, notice that we get a funny noise when we block the nose, and this noise appears as we produce the vowel sound /a/, not only when we produce the nasal consonant /n/.

Since it is predictable in English that we will only find nasal vowels before nasal consonants, we do not find any examples of words like *cat* produced with a nasal vowel. For a monolingual English speaker, it is difficult to produce the word *cat* with a nasal vowel, since that does not follow the English pattern. Try to see if you can do it.

Native speakers of English thus typically face difficulty mastering oral and nasal vowels in Brazilian Portuguese, a language in which it is not predictable where these sounds will occur. The word *vi*, meaning "I saw," is distinguished in sound from the word *vim*, meaning "I came," only in that *vi* has an oral vowel and *vim* has a nasal vowel.

Acquisition experiments have shown that children originally perceive a distinction not only among all possible speech sounds, but that they perceive a distinction that may be produced but is not perceptible by adult speakers of their language. As they learn their language(s), they lose the distinctions that do not play a role in their language(s).

For example, children raised in an English-speaking environment at six months distinguish the two sounds in English /ta/ and /da/, as do English-speaking adults. However, children at this stage also make distinctions that adults do not. In languages such as Hindi, there are four distinct /d/ sounds: "dental d," pronounced with the tongue touching the back of the teeth, symbolized in written Hindi as द, and "retroflex d," pronounced as English /d/ except with the tongue touching a little further back, symbolized in written Hindi as ड, and each of these also has a distinct version produced with a small puff of air—ध for the dental /d/ with a puff of air, and ढ for the retroflex /d/ with a puff of air. For a native speaker of Hindi, these distinctions are natural and obvious; to an adult native speaker of English, they are imperceptible.

However, English-speaking babies at six months do perceive the distinction between these different types of /d/ sounds that adults do not, as seen in a study by Werker (1989). When English-speaking ten-month-olds are tested, however, they do not show a perception in the distinction between these sounds.

5.3 Experimental Methods in Language Acquisition

Linguists have hypothesized that a significant portion of our language is in-born, and hence children are equipped at birth with many of the properties of our linguistic system. How can we determine whether this is the case? Newborns are typically not interested in conversations regarding the abstract structure of their language. In this section, we discuss three procedures which researchers use to discover what young children know about language: the high-amplitude sucking procedure, the preferential looking technique, and the head-turn preference procedure.

5.3.1 High-Amplitude Sucking Procedure

The high-amplitude sucking (HAS) procedure is one of the few techniques available, along with other physiological measures and brain scans, for studying language in newborns (see Floccia, Christophe, & Bertoncini, 1997). Infants must be awake in an alert state before the beginning of the study. They are placed in a comfortable reclined bath chair and are offered a sterilized pacifier that is connected to a pressure transducer and a computer via a piece of rubber tubing. Once the infant has begun sucking, the computer measures the infant's average sucking amplitude, or the strength of the infant's sucks. Following this baseline period, a sound is presented to the infant every time a strong or "high amplitude" suck is delivered. Infants quickly learn that their sucking controls the sounds, and they will suck more strongly and more often to hear the sounds. Infants' sucking rate over time can also be measured, to see if an infant "notices" when new sounds are played. A video from Werker (2014) shows how this method is used in language-learning experiments and introduces the two other techniques that I will describe.

Researchers have pointed out that the HAS procedure provides evidence that infants who are only one or two days old can differentiate an image of their mother from another woman. Babies sucking on a pacifier exposed to a picture of their mother suck harder in order to keep the picture in view, whereas when they are exposed to a picture of another woman with the same complexion, hair and eye color, and hairstyle, they do not suck as hard in order to keep the picture in view (Walton, Bower, & Bower, 1992).

5.3.2 Preferential Looking Technique

This technique is often called looking-while-listening. It is used to assess infants' word or sentence comprehension. Infants are typically presented with images of two objects side by side on a screen, while hearing a word or sentence that refers to one of the objects. The proportion of time that the infant looks at each of the images is measured. If infants increase their attention to the named object, then this is evidence that they were able to understand the word or sentence. Infants' looking after the word or sentence is often compared to their looking during a baseline period (either silent or with a neutral sentence, e.g. *Look at that!*) as infants sometimes show a pre-existing preference for looking at one image over another.

By six months, infants look at their mom longer when they hear *mom*, and look at their dad longer when they hear *dad*. This is long before they will regularly produce these sounds in association with these individuals.

5.3.3 Head-Turn Preference Procedure

The preferential looking technique that was described above has been used to show how infants perceive all contrasting speech sounds. It is typically used with babies between 5 and 12 months old. This procedure makes use of the fact that babies are interested in a moving toy, such as a monkey that claps cymbals together. Using the presentation of the moving toy as a reward, babies can be trained to turn their heads when they hear a change in a sound being presented. First, a sound is played over and over, and then the sound is changed, followed by activation of the toy monkey that is otherwise concealed. The babies turn to look at the monkey when it is activated. After several trials, when the sound being presented changes, the babies turn their heads toward the place where the monkey will appear even before it is activated.

Babies are trained using sound pairs that we know they can discriminate, and then they are presented new sound pairs to see whether they can discriminate the new contrast. Babies sit on their mothers' laps for this procedure, but the mothers wear headsets to prevent them from hearing the sounds and inadvertently providing cues to the babies (the Clever Hans effect). A researcher is also in the testing room to get the baby's attention between trials so that the baby is not already looking toward where the toy will appear before the stimuli are presented.

Using this procedure, researchers have shown that English-learning babies can discriminate vowel contrasts that are present in French but not in English (Trehub, 1976).

5.3.3.1 How Children Learn Words

Linguists are interested in finding out how young infants start to learn the meanings of words well before they start to produce these words. Researchers have made use of the head-turn preference procedure in this work. In an experiment by Jusczyk and Hohne (1997), the researchers visited the homes of eight-month-old babies over the course of two weeks. During each visit, the researchers would sit each infant in a seat and play a tape-recording of someone reading a story. As the babies were listening, they flipped through a book with pictures related to the story. Each of the ten visits took 30 minutes.

One set of words was used 13 times per visit (story words), and another set of words was not used at all (foils). At the end of the ten-day period, the researchers waited two weeks to return to the infants' homes. They then utilized the head-turn preference procedure technique to investigate if the infants would discriminate between words that they had heard in the story-telling sessions from words that they had not heard.

The researchers found that infants attended significantly more to words that they had been exposed to in previous sessions than to words that they had not been exposed to, even though it had been two weeks since the last story time. The findings suggest that eight-month-olds are beginning to engage in long-term storage of words that occur frequently in speech, long before they are able to produce any words.

5.4 Second Language Acquisition

Thus far in our discussion of language learning, we have been concerned with the child's acquisition of their first language. We may wonder whether language learning as an adult is significantly different from language learning as a child. Researchers have investigated the properties and patterns of second language acquisition in order to determine the answer to this question.

Note that the term "second language acquisition" is imprecise; a child may be exposed to French from birth until six months and then be exposed to Chinese. Although, technically speaking, Chinese is a second language for this child, this individual will be indistinguishable from someone exposed to Chinese from birth. Therefore, when researchers speak of second language acquisition, they are referring to the acquisition of a non-native language.

One way in which learning a second language is different from learning a first language is that people acquiring a second language have already learned a language from birth. They do not come to the second language as "empty slates," but have instead already acquired their native language.

We might wonder then if the native language plays an important role in the acquisition of a second language. Do second language learners start learning a non-native language with the unconscious assumption that their second language is going to be structured the same as their first language? We can explore this topic by investigating whether it is more difficult for second language learners to learn properties of the second language which differentiate this language from their first, while perhaps finding it more easy to learn properties that the two languages have in common (see Eubank, 1993/94).

5.4.1 Second Language Learning of the Sound System

Recall that we saw that children at the beginning of life have the capacity to learn all of the sounds of all of the languages of the world. Young infants perceive distinctions between different sounds that are not used in their language—distinctions that their parents cannot perceive. Unfortunately for us, this period does not last very long. Before they turn one year old, children are already differentiating the sound patterns that occur in their language versus those that do not.

We recognize that when we learn a language after 13, typically the sound system does not end up identical to a native speaker's sound system. When listening to a second language speaker who learned that language after the age of 15, we can typically distinguish features of that person's language that make it different from a native speaker's language.

Consider the pronunciation of the sound /p/ at the beginning of words in English and Spanish. In English, this sound is produced with a little puff of air. Examples of these words would be *pill, party,* and *piece.* If you place a tissue or a candle in front of your mouth while you say these words, you will notice that the candle will flicker or the tissue move as you produce the /p/ sound.

However, Spanish words that begin with /p/ do not occur with this puff of air. A native speaker of Spanish will not see the candle flicker when producing words such as *pobre* "poor," *pan* "bread," or *por* "for."

Thus, it is natural for an English speaker learning Spanish to pronounce the Spanish /p/ the same way as the English /p/, with that puff of air. To see this, compare the English and Spanish pronunciations of the name *Pablo.* When this name is said with English pronunciation, there is a puff of air that goes along with the sound /p/. When this name is said in Spanish, there is no puff of air.

Second language acquisition researchers have investigated the production of consonants in English speakers learning Spanish and have noted that these speakers will typically produce Spanish words with the English-sounding /p/. However, over time and with practice, English speakers may learn the Spanish pronunciation for /p/.

5.4.2 Second Language Learning of Structure

Recall from our discussion in Chapter 2 that, although in many languages it is possible to form a negative sentence by adding a negative word before the verb, in English this is not the case:

(5.5)   ~~some varieties of~~

    a.   John left the room.
    b.   *John not left the room.

As we have discussed, in English we follow a complex rule for forming negative sentences—first we add a form of the helping verb *do,* next *do* takes the tense of the main verb *left,* which here would be past, and *left* appears without any tense, as *leave.*

(5.6)

    a.   John left the room.

    b.   John not left the room.

    c.   John do not left the room.

    d.   John did not leave the room.

    e.   John didn't leave the room.

It is unlikely that a native speaker of English will explain this process to you if you inquire about negative sentences (unless they have studied linguistics), and yet English speakers use this unconscious knowledge to form negative sentences every day.

Since speakers of a second language are not able to articulate their unconscious knowledge of language (which is a good thing for linguists, because we would no longer have jobs), researchers develop techniques for assessing their linguistic knowledge.

Recall from our discussion above that in the learning of English negation, children pass through several stages, repeated here:

(5.7)

    No at the front of the sentence: *No I want juice.*

(5.8)

    No precedes the verb: *I no want juice.*

(5.9)

    Correct placement of negation: *I don't want juice.*

Larsen-Freeman and Long (1991) have shown that adults learning English as a non-native language seem to pass through the same stages, which they illustrate with the following examples:

(5.10) *No* at the front of the sentence:

No this one.

No you playing here.

(5.11) *No* precedes the verb:

She no has job.   *grammatical*

(5.12) Correct placement of negation:

I can't play the guitar.

She doesn't drink alcohol.

What conclusions can we draw from the parallel sequence of the acquisition of negation in native and non-native languages? Although we experience learning a non-native language very differently from learning our native language, which happens without any effort on our part, there are significant similarities between the unconscious processes of first and second language learning (Broselow & Finer, 1991; Bley-Vroman, Felix, & Ioup, 1988).

5.4.2.1 Grammaticality Judgment Task

A grammaticality judgment task is an experiment designed to discover which sentences sound like natural, normal sentences to speakers of a language. Using this method, theoreticians and experimentalists gather data to determine the syntax of a language. For example, in English, it is possible to have the sentence:

(5.13)

Richard brought Wilem to the beach.

However, if we were to scramble the words of this sentence and produce it as the following, this would no longer sound like a natural sentence of English:

(5.14)

*Beach Wilem the Richard to brought.

If someone were to approach you and utter (5.14), you would probably be taken aback, and you might wonder, "Why is this person speaking this way to me?" (Recall from Chapter 1 that linguists indicate that sentences such as (5.14) are unacceptable by marking them with a star (*).)

Notice that it is possible to have a sentence which is perhaps odd in its meaning but is still an acceptable, normal sentence of English. For example, consider the sentence in (5.15):

(5.15)

The ferocious lawyer gobbled up the jury and the Queen.

The meaning of this sentence is odd—it is difficult to imagine a lawyer gobbling up a jury and a Queen. However, even though the meaning of the sentence is strange, we still recognize it as a possible sentence of English. In contrast, what if we reversed the order of the words in this sentence? We would have (5.16):

(5.16)

*Queen the and jury the up gobbled lawyer ferocious the.

This sentence is surely deserving of a star for unacceptability—it would be quite a challenge to figure out what a person saying (5.16) had intended to express. Likewise, sentences may have an unlikely and infelicitous meaning, and yet be perfectly formed sentences of English:

(5.17)

Colorless green ideas sleep furiously.

This sentence has been discussed in the linguistics literature for decades. (See Marcus, 2012 for interesting discussion of this sentence.)

Linguists utilize grammaticality judgments to determine the structures and processes of language. Second language acquisition researchers want to understand how a second language learner goes about acquiring their non-native language. Do second language learners progress in learning the language by random trial and error, until they eventually learn the new system? Or do second language learners progress through systematic and predictable stages on their way to learning a non-native language?

One way to investigate what second language learners know about their language is to present them with sentences that are acceptable sentences for native speakers and those that are unacceptable for native speakers. If the second language learner shows a pattern of acceptability and unacceptability that is similar to a native speaker of the language, then that is evidence that they are acquiring a systematic syntax of their non-native language.

In an experiment on the acquisition of English as a non-native language by native Spanish speakers, White (1985) investigated the second language acquisition of subjects in English. Notice that English is a language which requires the presence of a subject for each sentence, as shown in (5.18a) and (5.18b) versus (5.18c):

(5.18)

    a.   Altea Paz won the race.

    b.   She won the race.

    c.   *Won the race.

When the subject of the sentence is a name such as *Altea Paz*, it typically occurs first in the sentence. If we use a pronoun for the subject, as in (5.18b), this subject *she* appears in initial position. However, if we try to produce this sentence without using the subject *she*, this sentence sounds strange in English.

However, notice that many languages of the world seem to follow a different pattern from English with respect to the behavior of subjects. For example, if we were to translate the three sentences in (5.19) into Spanish, we would have the following:

(5.19)

    a.   *Altea Paz   ganó   la   carrera.*
        Altea Paz   won   the   race
        "Altea Paz won the race."

    b.   *Ganó   la   carrera.*
        Won   the   race.
        "She/he won the race."

When the word *ella* "she" is included in the sentence as in (5.20), it is usually used to indicate emphasis of some sort.

(5.20)

Ella	*ganó*	*la*	*carrera.*
She	won	the	race

"<u>She</u> won the race."

So why is it possible to say *Ganó la carrera* in Spanish, meaning, "She/he won the race," whereas this sentence is not possible in English? As speakers of Spanish and many other languages know, Spanish has endings that appear on the verb that give the information about who the subject of the sentence is. We thus call languages such as Spanish "null-subject" languages.

White explored whether native speakers of Spanish would detect that the sentence *Won the race* sounds unacceptable in English. She found that a significant number of L2 learners of English (non-native speakers of English) rated the sentence as "acceptable." White wanted to know whether the acceptance of the sentence without the subject was due to Spanish-speakers' first language having the property of having null subjects. In order to investigate this, White made use of native speakers of French.

French patterns like English with respect to the presence of the subject, as is shown in (5.21):

(5.21)

j'ai gagné	"I won"	*nous avons gagné*	"we won"
tu as gagné	"you won"	*vous avez gagné*	"you (formal) won"
elle/il a gagné	"she/he won"	*elles/ils ont gagné*	"they won"

It is not possible in French to leave the pronominal subject of the sentence out, as shown below:

(5.22)

Altea Paz	*a gagné*	*la*	*course.*
Altea Paz	won	the	race.

"Altea Paz won the race."

(5.23)

Elle	*a gagné*	*la*	*course.*
She	won	the	race.

"She won the race."

(5.24)

*A gagné	*la*	*course.*
Won	the	race.

White showed that the French speakers behave differently from Spanish speakers—they do not rate the sentence without the subject as "acceptable." This seems to indicate that the properties of the native language make a crucial difference in the acquisition of a non-native language. It seems that learners of a new language initially hypothesize that their second language will have the structural properties of their first language. In the case of French learners learning English, this hypothesis is correct, and learners do not need to learn that it is not possible in English to leave the subject of the sentence out. However, speakers of Spanish hypothesize that English, like Spanish, allows a null subject, and therefore find sentences such as *Won the race* to be acceptable.

5.4.2.2 Sentence-Matching Experiment

Researchers have developed experimental methods in addition to grammaticality judgments in order to determine the processes and generalizations of second language acquisition. The sentence-matching experiment has the benefit that it is able to access the knowledge of grammar of second language speakers without asking for an overt judgment on a sentence (see Duffield, Matsuo, & Roberts, 2007). It taps into the unconscious knowledge that speakers have of their (native or non-native) grammar. In this method, subjects are presented pairs of sentences on a computer screen. The task of the subject is to determine whether the two sentences are the same or different.

For example, native speakers press the response button "yes" for the pair of sentences in (5.25) and they press the response "no" for the sentences in (5.26), because they are not identical.

(5.25) Pair of sentences that are identical:

Ella forgot the pie.   Ella forgot the pie.

(5.26) Pair of sentences that are not identical, both grammatical:

Cathy brought some bagels.   Cathy brought bagels.

Compare this with pairs of sentences which are unacceptable. Native speakers take a longer time to press the response button "yes" for the pair of sentences in (5.27) versus the sentences in (5.25), because the sentences in (5.27) are unacceptable. Likewise, speakers take longer to press the "no" response for the sentences in (5.28) versus (5.26) because the sentences are unacceptable.

(5.27) Pair of sentences that are ungrammatical and the same:

Ruth eats slowly her food.   Ruth eats slowly her food.

(5.28) Pairs of sentences that are ungrammatical and different:

Mary ate large an apple.   Mary ate an apple large.

The generalization that researchers have discovered is that native speakers of a language take longer to perform this task when the sentences are unacceptable, whereas when the sentences are acceptable, native speakers take less time to come to this conclusion (this is measured in milliseconds).

The idea is that if L2 learners are presented with pairs of sentences which are acceptable, they should take less time to respond to the sentences being the same or different than they would take when presented with sentences that are unacceptable, just as native speakers do. This indicates that they have knowledge of the contrast in acceptability of the pairs of sentences. This experimental design has the benefit that it does not require a subject to make an overt grammaticality judgment but rather detects this indirectly.

A study which utilizes this experimental methodology is the second language acquisition of medial causative constructions in French by Duffield, White, Bruhn de Garavito, and Montrul (2002). Native speakers of English who learn French as a second language are investigated in this experiment. The medial causative construction in French is illustrated in (5.29). Note that the object of the verb *fais* "made" in French, *le* "him", appears before the verb *fais*. As we can see in (5.30), this word order is not possible in English—the object of the English verb *made* is required to appear after the verb, as in (5.31). Example (5.32) shows that this word order is not possible in French.

(5.29)

Je	*le*	*fais*	*courir*
I	him	made	run

"I made him run."

(5.30)

*I him made run.

(5.31)

I made him run.

(5.32)

*Je	*fais*	*le*	*courir*
I	made	him	run

"I made him run."

We thus have a syntactic contrast between these two structures in French and English. Duffield et al. (2002) investigate the second language learning of these constructions in French. Since English does not allow this order, if it were the case that English speakers were relying on English structures to learn French, the L2 learners should behave differently from the native speakers.

　　The researchers discovered that both native speakers of French and L2 non-native speakers of French took longer to determine if two sentences with these constructions were the same sentences or not if the two sentences were unacceptable. We therefore have reliable ways to tap the unconscious knowledge of language that L2 learners have that does not rely on their grammaticality judgments.

5.5 Conclusion

In addition to relying on natural production for learning about how first and second language learners acquire their languages, language scientists have come up with several fascinating ways to learn about how this process works. Specialists in first language acquisition utilize the high-amplitude sucking procedure, preferential looking technique, and head-turn preference procedure. Scientists of second language learning make use of the grammaticality judgment task and sentence-matching experiment to learn about the unconscious acquisition of a non-native language.

Suggested Materials and Resources

For discussion of recent experimental methods in first language acquisition, see Ambridge and Rowland (2013).

A clear overview of experimental methods in language acquisition is provided in Flynn and Martohardjono (1995), Martohardjono and Flynn (1995), and Abugaber-Bowman, D. (2014).

Saville-Troike and Barto (2017), Berwick and Chomsky (2011), Kanno (2009), Schwartz (1999), and Gair and Martohardjono (1993) provide in-depth discussion of the generative approach to second language acquisition.

CHAPTER 6

Abnormal Language

6.1 Introduction

In our discussion of language learning in Chapter 5, we assumed that the language learner—the child or the adult—is provided with a normal context for language learning and use. A physically healthy person in an environment of language speakers is predicted to pass through the stages of language development that we explored. In this chapter, we investigate instances in which either an individual is not physically healthy, because of brain damage, or does not have a "normal environment," due to language deprivation. In order to discover what humans require in order to develop language normally, linguists investigate the result of physical damage or an insufficient environment—this leads to what linguists refer to as "abnormal language."

We take a close look at four instances of abnormal language. Cases of brain damaged individuals who suffer from language impairment provide insight into the particular areas of the brain that are implicated in language. Other individuals with language impairment have a condition from birth called Specific Language Impairment. These cases shed light on our understanding of the relationship between linguistic capacity and general cognitive capacity. Children who are raised in an environment in which language is lacking allow us to explore the effect of language deprivation on human development. We will also discuss an individual who is considered to be exceptionally gifted in language learning, a "language savant."

6.2 Language and the Brain

Recent research in the study of the brain has yielded fascinating results in several domains. With respect to language, scientists have discovered that particular areas of the brain are utilized for specific language functions. This provides evidence for the view that language is comprised of a modular system—there is a specific domain for the sounds of language, another domain for the structure of sentences, and yet another for the representation of meaning. We discuss here some of the exciting research that neurolinguists have conducted in order to determine the representation of language in the brain.

6.2.1 Brain Scans

Since we cannot see directly into our brains, we cannot observe its behavior in order to learn about how it works. Therefore, scientists develop ways to obtain access to what is happening inside the brain. An x-ray of the brain is able to show the blood vessels that run through it, but in order to investigate the brain in more detail, researchers make use of brain scans. One type of brain scan commonly used in neurolinguistics research is the fMRI. fMRI stands for functional Magnetic Resonance Imaging. In this technique, activity within the brain is measured. Since brain areas which are more active have increased blood flow, by measuring the amount of oxygen that is present in different parts of the brain (and which hence has more blood flow), we understand which parts of the brain are activated during a given activity.

In an fMRI scan of someone hearing a story, the language area of the brain in the left hemisphere (the superior temporal gyrus, or STG) is "lit up" because the person is participating in language behavior.

6.2.2 Compound Words in the Brain

In an influential in the journal *Brain and Language*, researchers investigated the brain's processing of different types of compound words (Boylan, Trueswell, & Thompson-Schill, 2017). Recall from discussion in Chapter 4 that compound words are words made up of two words, such as *blackboard* or *mountain lion*. (Compound words are sometimes written in English as a single word, but may be written as two words, or as connected by a dash as in *warm-blooded*.)

Boylan et al. (2017) point out that English has different types of compounds. The first type of compound is one in which the first word gives information about the second word, such as *container ship*, which is a ship for containers. Examples of this sort are *fish tank*, a tank for fish, and *water tank*, which is a tank for water. We also have compound words in English in which the first word is related to the second in a more complicated way: for example, *greenhouse* refers to a place for growing plants, not a house which is green. Another example of this type of compound is *redhead*, which does not refer to a head which is red, but rather a person who has red hair, or *lake house*, which does not refer to a house which is "a house for a lake," but rather a house which is located close to a lake.

On first inspection, these two different types of compound words in English look quite similar to each other. In fact, Boylan et al. show that these two groups are processed differently in the brain: while processing type 1 compounds, where the first word gives information about the second word, subjects' brains showed more activity in the anterior gyrus portion of the brain than when subjects were processing type 2 compounds (see Dowling, 2017 for an introduction to the anatomy of the brain).

Brain studies such as this one provide evidence that the way that our brains process language is sensitive to very specific differences in the meanings between words. The brain is designed to automatically differentiate between different shades of meaning that we have to pause and consciously think about in order to understand.

6.3 Aphasia

Aphasia is a brain disorder that results in problems in the understanding and production of language. Depending on which area of the brain is affected, the linguistic deficits of the patient vary. The foundational knowledge of neurolinguistics comes from the study of people who have undergone brain damage, as the result of an event such as a stroke or traumatic injury.

6.3.1 Broca's Aphasia

Paul Broca was a French surgeon who in 1861 observed a patient, Louis Victor Leborgne, over several years. Leborgne was able to understand French, but was unable to speak. After Leborgne passed away, an autopsy of his brain showed extensive damage to the fronto-temporal area of the brain, what is now known as Broca's area.

Here is a description of a picture shown to a patient who suffers from Broca's aphasia. In the picture, a woman is washing dishes in a kitchen while the sink overfills with water and two children who are in the background are stealing cookies.

(6.1)

> The woman is dishes ... I can dis ... the rest ... the dishes are filled with water ... the water floods ... the dishes or are floods ... the dishes are on ... the dishes are floods ... what's it's children children ... taking it the woman ... and the man children.

(Salis, 2006)

What seems to be missing from this speech? The person seems to want to say "The woman is <u>washing</u> the dishes ..." Note that the patient's speech is filled with hesitations and pauses. Much of her speech is indecipherable: "I can dis ... the rest ...," although sections are interpretable, "The dishes are filled with water." Typically patients with Broca's aphasia show physical difficulty producing speech.

6.3.2 Wernicke's Aphasia

Carl Wernike was a neuropsychiatrist in Germany who studied individuals who had suffered language difficulties after undergoing damage to their brain. These individuals appeared quite different from the patient who Paul Broca had worked with. These individuals had difficulty understanding language, although their hearing was normal. However, unlike Broca's patient, these patients were able to speak fluently. In these patients, the brain had suffered damage in the posterior region, which therefore came to be known as Wernicke's area.

Compare the following description of the same picture of the woman washing dishes that was discussed above. Recall that in the picture, a woman is washing dishes in a kitchen while the sink over-fills with water and two children who are in the background are stealing cookies.

(6.2)

> Uh, we're in the in the kermp kerken kitchen in in the kitchen and there's a lady doing the slowing ... she's got the pouring the plate watching it with with um ... the water is balancing in the sink the (unintelligible) of the sink and the water is pouring all over the bowing bowing all over it.

(Edwards, 2005)

How does this description sound different from the Broca's aphasic? In terms of the structure of the sentences, everything seems to be normal—this sounds like fluent speech. However, when we attend to the meanings of the words, we realize that much of what the patient says does not combine together to form a coherent meaning.

Patients who suffer from Wernicke's aphasia have speech that sounds fluent, but the meaning does not seem be appropriate. On the other hand, those who have Broca's aphasia seem to have great difficulty expressing language.

6.4 Specific Language Impairment (SLI)

Just as the study of people with particular forms of brain damage helped scientists to understand the representation of language in the brain, the investigation of people who suffer from a genetic language disorder can shed light on how language is represented in the mind. Specific Language Impairment (SLI) is a syndrome that leads to particular problems with language. People with SLI have normal intelligence, but have difficulties with the structure of words and sentences. The language problems associated with SLI often involve grammatical areas such the ones that we discussed in Chapter 5 when talking about language learning. Recall that these grammatical elements are, for example, verb endings and the plural marker *-s* in the plural form *hats*. As you can see from the examples below, it is possible to have an impairment in these areas of grammar without any apparent difficulty in the expression of meaning (see Gopnik & Crago, 1991; Gopnik, 1994; Crago & Gopnik, 1994). These are sentences uttered by a patient with SLI:

(6.3)

   a.   It's a flying finches, they are.
   b.   She remembered when she hurts herself the other day.
   c.   The neighbors phone the ambulance because the man fall off the tree.
   d.   The boys eat four cookie.
   e.   Carol is cry in the church.
   f.   It's something white but I can't find.

Although the meaning of each of these expressions is clear, there is something missing or incorrect in the forms of the words. For example, in (a), the sentence would be well-formed if it were *They are flying finches, they are.* Thus, we can understand SLI as a disruption in the representation of language in the brain. Given that this does not correlate with general cognitive ability, this disorder supports the view that language is located in a specific and independent position in the mind.

6.5 Stuttering

It is important to distinguish SLI from problems involving articulation, such as stuttering. Stuttering typically involves a problem in the physical production of language, while people with SLI may show difficulty with the general use of language. It is crucial that young children facing a language problem be properly diagnosed, since the treatment for SLI is different from that for stuttering.

   According to Logan (2015), stuttering involves a repetition of sounds, syllables, words, or phrases, prolongation of sounds, and interruptions in speech. An individual who stutters is aware of what they want to say, but they are unable to produce speech in the way they intend.

Guitar (2013) provides the following examples of stuttering:

(6.4)

    a.   *W- W- W- Where are you going?*

        Part-word repetition: The person is having difficulty moving from the /w/ in *where* to the remaining sounds in the word. On the fourth attempt, she successfully completes the word.

    b.   *SSSS ave me a seat.*

        Sound prolongation: The person is having difficulty moving from the /s/ in *save* to the remaining sounds in the word. He continues to say the /s/ sound until he is able to complete the word.

    c.   *I'll meet you – uummm uuummm you know like – around six o'clock.*

        A series of interjections: The person expects to have difficulty smoothly joining the word *you* with the word *around*. In response to the anticipated difficulty, she produces several interjections until she is able to say the word *around* smoothly.

Linguists have argued that SLI and stuttering provide evidence for the view that language is biologically separate from our general cognitive capacities, such as intelligence and memory, since people who have these disorders do not suffer from low intelligence or other cognitive problems. People with these disorders are aware of their behavior and how it is different from others.

6.6 Language Isolation

6.6.1 Genie

Genie is a girl who was discovered at the age of 13, after having suffered tragic abuse. From approximately 18 months onward, she had lived tied to a chair in a darkened room. She was frequently beaten and never spoken to. When she was discovered by a social worker, she could not stand erect, had no speech and had the general cognitive capacity of a one-year-old.

According to Curtiss (1978), Genie entered the Children's Hospital Los Angeles where a team of psychiatrists, psychologists, and linguists were organized to evaluate and help her. Although she was initially almost silent, Genie later learned to express herself and communicate with those around her. She went from a very withdrawn person to someone who enjoyed socializing with others. Genie enjoyed listening to classical music played on the piano—researchers speculated that she may have been able to hear a neighborhood child practicing to play piano while she was isolated.

Genie was given intensive language therapy for many years. She was able to learn new words, particularly lexical items such as nouns and verbs, but had difficulty acquiring function words, such as articles and prepositions, as well. Genie was able to learn the sounds of English, but she was not able to master normal English intonation.

The two areas in which Genie showed the greatest deficits, even after years of intensive instruction and practice, were syntax (sentence structure) and pragmatics (language use proper to a particular situation). She achieved a very limited knowledge of sentence structure and often produced utterances with an ungrammatical word order. Typical expressions were the following:

(6.5)

    a.   Genie full stomach.
           "I have a full stomach."
    b.   Mama have baby grow up.
           "Mama has a baby who grew up."
    c.   Father hit Genie cry long time ago.
           "When my father hit me, I cried, a long time ago."
    d.   Applesauce buy store.
           "Buy applesauce at the store."
    e.   Man motorcycle have.
           "The man has a motorcycle."

Genie was not able to master social conventions of language, such as *hello, please,* and *thank you.* Notice that these conventions depend on one's awareness of social context—it seems that Genie was not able to fully develop normal language behavior.

Linguists hypothesize that there is a critical period for language acquisition. From birth until about 12 or 13, children exposed to a language can become native speakers of the language. If we learn a language after this age, the effortless, automatic acquisition process of childhood does not take place. Since Genie was discovered beyond the critical period, she did not have available this automatic and unconscious process of learning. Her tragic case thus provides evidence for the view that certain aspects of language are only able to develop if normal exposure takes place within this critical period of development.

6.6.2 Chelsea

There is another case of extreme lack of exposure to language which has been discussed in the literature on language development. Chelsea is a partially deaf woman who was from a loving, supportive home. However, Chelsea was incorrectly diagnosed as retarded at birth, and had therefore never been exposed to a signed language. Her language handicap was believed by her family to be due to her retardation.

At the age of 31, it was discovered that Chelsea was partially deaf, and she began to wear hearing aids. After intensive therapy, Chelsea was able to learn many words and her intonation sounded normal. Chelsea also mastered social conventions such as *hello, how are you?,* etc.

Although she attained a large vocabulary, Chelsea's syntax and morphology were more problematic than Genie's (Curtiss, 1988, 1989a, 1989b). As the following examples illustrate, her utterances were structurally abnormal:

(6.6)

    a.   They are is car in the Tim.

    b.   Breakfast eating girl.

    c.   The small a the hat.

d.   Orange Tim car in.

e.   I Wanda be drive come.

f.   Airplane fly headache.

g.   Combing hair the boy.

h.   Daddy are be were to the work.

Unlike Genie, there seems to be a complete lack of regular word order from which the meaning of the sentence can be obtained. However, Chelsea, unlike Genie, was able to learn fixed expressions and socially appropriate expressions.

This difference in the ultimate language attainment of Genie and Chelsea can be explained given the Critical Period Hypothesis. Because Genie was discovered very close to the end of the critical period of learning, she was able to acquire a more regular system of sentence structure and word structure. The fact that she was unable to learn the socially appropriate use of language may be due to her extremely socially deprived life before discovery. On the other hand, Chelsea was not discovered until well beyond the critical period of acquisition, and therefore never mastered a normal system of language structure; however, the fact that she had had a socially normal childhood made it possible for her to learn the social aspects of language that Genie could not.

6.7 A Language Savant

The two examples of unusual language deprivation that we have discussed, Genie and Chelsea, provide examples of circumstances in which individuals were prevented from learning a language until they were beyond the critical period of language acquisition. In this section, we turn to an example of an individual who seems to be extraordinarily gifted in learning language.

The movie *Rain Man* featured a savant (previously called *idiot savant*, the French for "knowledgeable idiot"), a person who although extremely gifted in one area of cognitive development, is generally cognitively underdeveloped. Savants have been studied in the areas of mathematics, music, art, and memory.

Christopher was the first person with a special capacity in learning languages to be discovered and investigated by linguists. He can read, write, and communicate in any of 15 to 20 languages, from a wide typological range and written in a number of different scripts. As described by Neil Smith and Ianthi Tsimpli in their book, *The Mind of a Savant: Language, Learning and Modularity*, Christopher was diagnosed with brain damage when he was very young (Smith & Tsimpli, 1995). At about age three, Christopher took an enthusiastic interest in factual books, such as dictionaries and books about flags. His language developed, along with an unusual ability to easily read when materials were presented upside down or sideways. When Christopher was about six years old, he started to become interested in books and papers written in other languages.

Smith and Tsimpli (1995, p. 18) provide an example of Christopher's ability to pick up languages quickly: shortly before Christopher was planning to appear on Dutch television, "It was suggested that he might spend a couple of days improving his rather rudimentary Dutch with the aid of a grammar and dictionary. He did so to such good effect that he was able to converse in Dutch—with facility if not total fluency—both before and during the program."

Smith and Tsimpli performed a fascinating experiment in order to discover if Christopher, an individual with an advanced language learning capacity, would be able to learn a language which violated principles of Universal Grammar (UG). Recall from our discussion in Chapter 4 that UG consists of principles which all human languages follow, and therefore it would be impossible for a human to learn a language which violates principles of UG.

Smith and Tsimpli set out to test this claim, by inventing a language which is similar to other human languages in all ways except that it violates certain rules of UG. They called this language "Epun," and they attempted to teach this "language" to Christopher, with the prediction that Christopher would be able to learn the language, except for the areas that were in violation of UG. In this way, they were able to investigate the prediction of Noam Chomsky from years earlier,

"Similarly, knowing something about Universal Grammar, we can readily design 'languages' that will be unattainable by the language faculty" (Chomsky, 1991, p. 40).

In order to understand how Smith and Tsimpli created this "impossible language," recall the discussion of the Principle of Structure Dependency from Chapter 4:

(6.7) Principle of Structure Dependency (Chomsky, 1971, p. 30):

All formal operations in the grammar of human language are dependent on the abstract structure of the sentence.

In our discussion of this principle, we attempted to devise a rule that would describe the process of Question Formation in English, illustrated in (6.8a–b).

(6.8)

a.   Wilem is viewing the stars.
b.   Is Wilem viewing the stars?

Based on these two sentences, we could formulate the rule of question formation as in (6.9):

(6.9) English Question Formation Rule (Version 1)

In order to form a question from a statement, switch the position of the first two words in the sentence.

Although elegant, this rule runs into the problem that it cannot account for the structure of other questions in English, such as:

(6.10)

The boy will leave the room.

If we apply the English Question Formation Rule to this sentence, we get (6.11):

(6.11)

*Boy the will leave the room?

Rather, the way that we would form the question would be:

(6.12)

Will the boy leave the room?

We could update our rule for forming questions in English by stating it as in (6.13):

(6.13) English Question Formation Rule—Version 2

In order to form a question from a statement, switch the position of the subject of the sentence with the auxiliary verb.

So, in the example in (6.12), the subject "the boy" switches position with the auxiliary verb "will." Since all processes of grammar are based on the abstract structure of the sentence, making use of such concepts as "subject" and "auxiliary verb," they cannot rely on, for example, the linear order of words in the sentence, as our first version of the Question Formation Rule required.

The language that Smith and Tsimpli created had all of the properties of a human language, except that it violated the Principle of Structure Dependency. For example, in Epun, the emphatic form of a sentence is formed by adding "nog" to the end of the *third word of the sentence*. Notice that this rule makes use of linear order as opposed to abstract syntactic structure, in violation of the Principle of Structure Dependency.

Smith and Tsimpli observe that although Christopher was able to learn processes of grammar in Epun which were structure-dependent, he was unable to master the rule for emphasis, indicating that his learning of Epun was in fact constrained by the Principle of Structure Dependency.

6.8 Conclusion

In this chapter, we have examined four domains in which language may be described as abnormal: (1) examples of brain damage which show that particular aspects of language are biologically represented in distinct areas of the brain; (2) Specific Language Impairment, which supports the claim that language develops independently of general intelligence; (3) children raised in an environment deprived of language showing that normal language learning must take place within a set period of human development; and (4) an example of a language savant, who was claimed to be unable to learn aspects of an invented language which violated universal principles of language.

Suggested Materials and Resources

Sacks (1998) is a well-regarded work of fiction that introduces leading ideas in neuroscience.

Rymer (1994) is a film that describes the discovery and experiences of Genie, introduced in this chapter. (Please be advised that this film describes in detail the extreme abuse and neglect that Genie suffered.)

CHAPTER 7

Bilingualism

I have never known what is Arabic or English, or which one was really mine beyond any doubt. What I do know, however, is that the two have always been together in my life, one resonating in the other, sometimes ironically, sometimes nostalgically, most often each correcting, and commenting on, the other. Each can seem like my absolutely first language, but neither is.

Edward Said (1999)

[handwritten annotation: LC you think there's one "first" LG]

If I speak only one language, I can help my country as only one man. If I can use two languages, I can help as two men. But if I can use all nine languages, then I can work as nine men. [Village Elder, Eritrea. Eritreans speak nine languages: Afar, Arabic, Bilen, Hedareb, Kunama, Nara, Soho, Tigre, and Tigrigna.]

Dutcher (1998)

7.1 Introduction

In previous generations, it was commonly believed that learning one language is the normal and natural way for acquisition to take place, and that learning more than one language would lead to cognitive confusion, lower intelligence, or to children growing up speaking no language properly. Linguists have noted that the claim that learning a single language is normal and natural seems to be contradicted by the fact that the world's population is by far multilingual, and that, in fact, perhaps monolingualism should be viewed as the exceptional language-learning situation. (In this reading, I will use the term *bilingualism*; however, all of the discussion holds for instances of trilingualism, etc.)

A long-standing question that linguists have investigated is, "How does the process of learning multiple languages take place?" It may seem plausible that in learning more than one language, each language is represented in a distinct location, and that multiple languages therefore develop in the manner that single languages do. However, we will see that studies of multilinguals provide us with a picture which is much more complex than this.

7.2 Models of Bilingualism

7.2.1 Unitary Language System Hypothesis

Volterra and Taeschner (1978) propose what they called the "Unitary Language System Hypothesis," according to which bilingual children progress through three separate stages of development.

7.2.1.1 Three Stages of Bilingual Development

(7.1)

a. In the first stage, the two languages share a single store of words (what linguists call the "lexicon"; this is our mental dictionary that provides a list of all of the words that we know and their sounds and meanings).

b. The second stage develops when children develop two separate lexicons, for each of the two languages, but still have one grammatical system for the two languages.

c. The third stage is the final stage of acquisition, at which point children have two completely separate lexicons and grammatical systems.

Evidence for the Unitary Language System Hypothesis seems to come from "mixed utterances"—utterances which include elements of

two different languages. A monolingual adult hearing a child producing sentences that contain some words from one language and some
words from another may conclude that what they are hearing is an
unprincipled mixing of the two languages. However, linguists have
investigated in detail what exactly language mixing consists in, and
have come to different conclusions.

7.2.1.2 Language Mixing

Hoffman (1995, chapter 4) provides examples of children learning English and Spanish who mix the two languages, such as in the
following examples from Mario, who is three and a half years old,
originally discussed in Fantini (1985, p. 5). (The complete Spanish
expressions are provided in parentheses.)

(7.2)

    a. Mario: *un juguete para el   baby* (*un juguete para el bebe*)
                a   toy   for   the baby
           "a toy for the baby"

    b. Mario: *Yo lo voy   a   lokar.* (*Yo lo voy a cerrar con llave.*)
                I   it am-going to lock
           "I am going to lock it."

    c. Mario: *Papa's zapatos*   (*los zapatos de Papa*)
                Papa's shoes

Notice that in the second example, Mario has used an English verb
lock instead of the Spanish form *cerrar con llave*, but that the form
that he uses for the verb is a Spanish form: *lokar*. In the third example,
Mario uses the Spanish words *papa* and *zapatos*, but inserts them
into an English structure, with the possessive -'s, which is not a
possible structure in Spanish.

    Several examples from an English–German bilingual child, pro-
duced from age two and a half to three years and eight months
include the following (Hoffman, 1995), with monolingual expressions
in parentheses:

(7.3)

   a.   *Tee schon ge<u>pour</u>*   (*Tee schon eingegossen.*)
       "Tea has been poured."

   b.   *play <u>mit</u> water*   (*play with water*)
       "play with water"

   c.   *And the froggie's getting <u>nass</u>.*   (*And the froggie's getting wet.*)
       "And the froggie's getting wet."

In the first example, the English verb *pour* is treated as a German verb, appearing with *ge-* at the beginning. The second example shows a child replacing a single word, the preposition *with*, for the German equivalent. The third example includes a sentence completely in English, except for the last word in German, *nass* "wet."

An example from a German–French bilingual child is the following, where the phrase meaning "for dog" is switched from German to French (Hoffman, 1995):

(7.4)

Das   ist   ein   Knochen   <u>pour</u>   <u>chien</u>.
That   is   a   bone   for   dog
"That is a bone for the dog."

An English–Arabic bilingual child produced the following, showing how a verb from one language, English *live*, may be treated as in the other language, Arabic, by placing the Arabic *be-* prefix at the front of it:

(7.5)

Huwa   be<u>live</u>   fii   ilghaabi.
He   lives   in   jungle
"He lives in the jungle."

What these examples reveal is that language mixing is systematic; in each example, a linguistic unit is affected, whether it is a word, or the stem of a word, or a whole phrase. In other words, children are manipulating the linguistic system in predictable and complex ways. What may appear at first glance to be confusion between two languages is in fact indicative of a highly systematic language process.

Why should children produce such mixed utterances? Hoffman claims that there may be several reasons for this:

(7.6)

- a.   If a word has been acquired in one language, and not yet in the other language, the child may insert the known word into the sentence.
- b.   When the child is speaking, they may not remember a particular word or phrase in the language that they are speaking, so they will say it in the other language.
- c.   Children learn from the language spoken around them. It is natural for a child growing up learning French and German, for example, to hear sentences in which a bilingual adult mixes the two languages. Therefore, it would be surprising if children did not produce utterances that are mixed.

7.2.2 Independent Development Hypothesis

In contrast to the Unitary Language System Hypothesis, which claims that bilingual children start the learning process with a single language system, Padilla and Liebman (1975) have proposed the Independent Development Hypothesis, according to which the two languages develop separately from the beginning of language learning.

Evidence for the Independent Development Hypothesis comes from the observation that bilingual children utilize the appropriate structures for the language that they are speaking.

For example, consider the following difference between English and German sentences:

(7.7)

- a.   English: (*John said that ...*) *I will read the book.*
- b.   German: (*John sagte, dass ...*) *ich   das   Buch   lessen   werde.*
         John   said   that ...   I   the   book   read   will
         "(John said that ...) I will read the book."

Notice that, in English, the word order of the second part of the sentence is *I will read the book*, whereas in German, the word order of this part of the sentence is *I the book read will*. Now consider what a German–English bilingual child should produce, if it is the case that there is a stage in their language development where they have a single structure for both languages. There should be sentences with English words but German structure, as in the example in (7.8a) below, and/or sentences with German words but English structure, as in (7.8b).

(7.8) Predicted Utterances:

a. (*John said that ...*) *I the book read will.*

b. (*John sagte, dass ...*) *ich werde lessen das Buch.*

In fact, researchers have argued that these types of examples do not occur in bilingual children's speech; the structure that children use when they speak one language is the correct structure for that language.

Consider another type of unattested example. Werner Leopold was a linguist who recorded the utterances of his two children as they learned both English and German, from 1939 to 1949. These longitudinal collections are known as "diary studies" (see Leopold, 1949) One difference between English and German is how to form questions. As discussed in Chapter 1, in English, we have the question formed from the statement as follows:

(7.9) English:

This can be a question

You want tea.

Do you want tea?

As we have discovered, in order to form a question in English, the auxiliary verb moves to the front of the sentence. If there is no auxiliary verb in the sentence, we use a form of the verb *do*.

In contrast, the formation of questions in German takes place as follows:

(7.10) German

    a.   *Sie wollen Tee.*

         "You want tea."

    b.   *Wollen*   *Sie*   *Tee?*

         want   you   tea

         "Do you want tea?"

There is no need to have an auxiliary verb in German to form questions; in this language, the main verb, for example, *wollen* "want", moves to the front of the sentence to form the question.

Given this difference between the two languages, one might expect Leopold to have observed at some point in the development of his two bilingual children a stage at which they would apply the structure of English questions to German, or the structure of German questions to English, in which case they would produce sentences such as the following:

(7.11) English question, German structure: *Not second La but bilingual-ism* [handwritten]

    Want you tea?

However, it seems that children in fact do not confuse these two processes in the two languages; Leopold claimed that there were no instances of this type of example in his children's speech.

Annick De Houwer's (1990, p. 338) investigation of the language development of an English–Dutch bilingual child, Kate, also supports the Independent Language Hypothesis. She claims that, "in all aspects of language use investigated that provided unambiguous opportunities for discovering either the presence or the absence of inter-linguistic interaction, we were able to show that Kate's developing knowledge of Dutch could not function as a basis of her speech production in English, or vice versa. Instead, Kate used Dutch devices while producing utterances with only Dutch words, and English devices when producing utterances with only English words."

7.3 Code-Switching

It is probably impossible to walk for more than ten minutes any-where in Miami without hearing conversation that mixes English and Spanish. In fact, code-switching is a very robust linguistic feature, found wherever there is a population of bilinguals.

Linguists use the term "code-switching" to refer to bilinguals' ability to mix their languages during communication. Bilinguals may switch languages within a conversation, or substitute a word or phrase from one language with a phrase or word from another language. A typical example of English–Spanish code-switching, in a bilingual child named Isabella (aged three), is discussed in Arias and Lakshmanan (2005, p. 98), shown below:

(7.12)

Mom:	No..which is your favorite color Isabella?
Isabella:	Mmmmm. Pink.
Mom:	Pink, wow.
Isabella:	*Mi duele a barriga.*
	"I have a stomachache."
Mom:	*¿Y por qué? Tienes hambre?*
	"Why? Are you hungry?"
Isabella:	*Sí.*
	"Yes"
Mom:	*Tienes hambre, vamos a hacer la comida ...*
	"You are hungry, let's make our meal ..."
Isabella:	*Tu duele la barriga?*
	"Do you have a stomachache?"
Mom:	*Sí, un poquito, porque yo tambien tengo hambre.*
	"Yes, a little bit, because I'm hungry too."
Isabella:	*A mí también.*
	"Me too."

Notice that Isabella switches from English to Spanish when she wants her mother to comfort her.

Code-switching across sentences is also illustrated in the Spanish–Hebrew example in (7.13), from Berk-Seligson (1986, p. 323), where Hebrew is underlined:

(7.13)

"No," díso el marído, "si afilú le van a kortár el pye a Malká, yo la vo tomár. Aní ikárti otá im ste regláyim."

"'No', said her husband, 'Even if they are going to cut off Malká's foot, I am going to take her. I knew her with two legs.'" *by who (m)?*

Interestingly, code-switching is often frowned upon. Common negative attitudes about code-switching are that "people who code-switch do not know how to speak one language fully," or that code-switching is "a mish-mash of two undeveloped languages." Depending on its context of use, the term "Spanglish" itself may be used with a pejorative meaning. It is therefore not surprising that people who engage in code-switching themselves may deny it; bilinguals who claim that they never mix languages in fact do code-switch. This suggests that code-switching is a natural process for bilinguals.

7.3.1 Code-Switching is Rule-Governed

Linguists have shown that code-switching is rule-governed; it may take place in only certain linguistic contexts. For example, a Spanish–English bilingual may produce a sentence such as the following, where the English noun *grandfather* is used.

(7.14)

Se lo di a mi grandfather.　　(*Se lo di a mi abuelo.*)
"I gave it to my grandfather."

However, bilinguals agree that the sentence below sounds odd, where the whole English phrase *my grandfather* is used:

(7.15)

*Se lo di a my grandfather.

Another example which illustrates this point is from Russian–English code-switching in (7.16); bilinguals of Russian and English agree that while (7.16a) would be a possible way to say this phrase, (7.16b) would not (example from Babyonyshev & Brun, 2004), with English underlined:

(7.16)

a.	*takoj*	*tixij*	<u>*quiet guy*</u>
	such-sg-masc-nom	quiet-masc-nom	quiet guy

"such a quiet quiet guy"

b.	**takoj*	<u>*quiet*</u>	*tixij*	<u>*guy*</u>
	such-sg-masc-nom	quiet	quiet-masc-nom	guy

"such a quiet quiet guy"

The Hindi–English code-switching examples in (7.17) illustrate the restrictions on this form of speech (from Di Sciullo, Muysken, & Singh, 1986, p. 17):

(7.17)

a. *I told him that <u>rām bahut bimār hai</u>.*
"I told him that Ram was very sick."

b. **I told him <u>ki rām bahut bimār hai</u>.*
"I told him that Ram was very sick."

In addition, speakers of Spanish and English agree that it is possible to switch languages with adverbials, such as *next week*; however, it is not possible to switch languages with question words, as shown in the contrast between the two following sentences:

(7.18)

a. *Vamos <u>next week</u>.*   (*Vamos la próxima semana.*)
"We will go next week."

b. **¿<u>When</u> vamos?*   (*¿Cuando vamos?*)
"When will we go?"

In addition, bilinguals may say the first sentence below, where the Spanish adjective *amistoso* is replaced with the English equivalent;

however, the version underneath, with the adverb *muy* replaced, sounds unnatural to bilinguals:

(7.19)

   a.   *Es muy friendly*   (*Es muy amistoso.*)
        "He is very friendly."

   b.   **Es very amistoso.*
        "He is very friendly."

The fact that there are linguistic generalizations about where it is that code-switching can take place shows that it is a linguistically complex, regular, rule-based behavior. Otherwise, we would expect to be able to find code-switching at any point in a conversation or sentence.

7.3.2 Why do Bilinguals Code-Switch?

Linguists have explored the question: What motivates a bilingual person to code-switch? If you are bilingual, in the next conversation that you have with another bilingual, try to keep track of the switches between your two languages (without telling the other person!), and try to think about why it is that the switch took place in each instance. In some cases, you may see that switching takes place when talking about a topic that is associated more with one language. For example, two English–Spanish bilinguals who speak mainly English at school and Spanish at home may switch from Spanish to English when talking about a topic related to something that happened at school, or may go from English to Spanish when describing an event that took place in the household.

It is commonly believed that bilinguals switch from one language to the other because they do not know a particular word or phrase in the language they are speaking. Zentella argues against this claim in chapter 5 of her book *Growing Up Bilingual* (1997). In a study of the language usage of a Spanish–English bilingual population in New York City, Zentella shows that, in the overwhelming majority of cases involving a switch in language (75%), the person who does the switch in fact does know how to say the expression in the other language. (She confirms that the person does know the expression by recording their conversations over a long period of time and hearing them use the expression correctly in that language.) In only 3% of the cases that she examined did the person not know the expression in the other language, and in another 3%, speakers reported to have temporarily forgotten how to say the word or phrase in the other language. (The rest of the examples were undetermined, because Zentella did not happen to record the speakers using the expression in the other language and thus could not positively know whether the speaker knew the expression or not.)

Zentella notes that bilingual children often change languages according to who they are speaking with and what their assumptions are about that person's language preference. She noted that the children in her study often speak to each other in English but to their family members in Spanish.

Zentella discusses what she calls "Non-Reciprocal Conversation." This is where one speaker is using one language, and the other speaker is using another language. The conversation may continue in this manner until it finishes. One reason for non-reciprocal conversation is that each speaker may choose to speak in the language in which they feel most comfortable conversing, although both speakers are able to fully understand everything said in the other language.

Code-switching serves many distinct functions in conversation, of which the bilinguals who use the switches might not be aware. Several motivations for code-switching that Zentella discussed are summarized here.

7.3.2.1 Changing the Topic

Changing the language may serve to change the topic of conversation among bilinguals, as seen in the following example:

(7.20)

> *Vamos a preguntarle. It's raining!*
> "Let's go ask her. It's raining!"

An example of code-switching in Korean and English from Yun (2005) with four young girls discussing rides on an amusement park illustrates this. Notice how the switch from Korean into English in C's second conversational contribution dramatically changes the topic to focus on what she is talking about.

(7.21)

A: *Hoksi, dariae hoksi daenungeo?*
"Probably, probably something attached on an ankle?"

B: *Ananja ikko tanunkeo?*
"The thing we don't sit and ride on?"

C: *Ani kugeo anya*
"No, not that."

A: *Anja itnundae itnundae darika bakuro naohnungeo?*
"While sitting, something that our legs are out of the ride?"
Kukeo kukeo nan kiga Great Whitegeo dun?
"My height fits in Great White."

C: *Nan paransaekira Datanungeo geodun*
"My ticket was blue so that I was able to ride on anything."

(...no one responds...)

I'M SPEAKING, PEOPLE!!!!
(Shouts while holding up her fists in the air)

D: *Ha, ha, ha, ha.*
(Loud laughing)

7.3.2.2 Marking quotations

It is very common to find code-switches at the beginning and end of direct quotes, regardless of the language that is actually used by the person who speaks. For example:

(7.22)

El me dijo, "Call the police!" pero yo dije, "No voy a llamar la policia nada."

"He said to me, 'Call the police!', but I said, 'I'm not going to call the police for nothing.'"

Code-switching between English and Afrikaans shows a similar behavior in the example in (7.23) (Van Dulm 2007, p. 64):

(7.23)

Dis soos "Thank you for giving me money,"
It-is like, "Thank you for giving me money,"
"It's like, 'Thank you for giving me money,'

hierso's jou geld nou.
here-is your money now
now here's your money."

7.3.2.3 Follow the Leader

Another strategy of code-switching is to switch to the other language when one of the conversational participants does. This is illustrated by the Cantonese Chinese–English code-switching example in (7.24). In this example from an English class, a student Jason begins in English and then switches to Cantonese. The teacher replies to him in English in order to keep the conversation in English, but Anita, Suzy, and Harry continue in Cantonese, following Jason's lead:

(7.24)

Jason:　　*Yellow, yellow, yellow. Pee pee, wo yao niao niao.*
　　　　　　　　　　　　　　　　"I want to go pee pee."

Teacher:　*Jason, you pee pee many times.*

Anita:　　*Teacher, wo yao ca biti.*
　　　　　　　"I want to wipe my nose."

Suzy:　　*wo ye yao.*
　　　　　　"Me too."

Harry:　　*Teacher, wo yao he shuei*
　　　　　　"I want to drink water."

Anita:　　*Teacher, wo yao he shuei*
　　　　　　"I want to drink water."

Suzy: *wo ye yao*
            "Me too."

7.3.2.4 Checking Listeners' Opinion

Switches are often found at the end of sentences in tags. The example in (7.25) illustrates this with an example in Spanish with an English tag, and (7.26), from Berk-Seligson (1986), shows this with a Spanish example that ends with a Hebrew tag:

(7.25)

¿Porque estamos en huelga de gasolina, right?
"Because we are in a gas strike, right?"

(7.26)

¿Se sta kitándo la káska entéra, naxón?
"One takes off the entire peel, right?"
(The sentence is in Spanish except for the last word *naxón*, in Hebrew.)

7.3.2.5 Changing the Story Structure

Switching languages may serve to deliver a punch line or provide an ending to a story. For example, from Zentella (1997) we find the following:

(7.27)

Charlie tried to push Gina in and, bendito, Kitty fell on her head. Y eso es lo que le pasa a los presentados como tu.
"Charlie tried to push Gina in and, poor her, Kitty fell on her head. And that's what happens to busybodies like you."

To answer the question "Why do bilinguals code-switch?", we might answer, "Because they can"—in other words, switching languages is one strategy that bilinguals have to achieve meanings that monolinguals use other strategies for. For example, how do monolinguals indicate a change in the conversational topic, as discussed above? They may use intonation, as in the following example.

Imagine that your friend Martha, who is always going on and on about her boyfriend and what a marvelous prince he is, is starting yet again to talk about him, and you are not in the mood to listen to it. Then the following might happen:

(7.28)

> Martha: ... So then he said, "Sweetie-pie, nothing is too good for my little angel ..."
>
> You: Yeah, well, what about our plans for Friday night?

Notice that the way you say "Yeah, well, what about our plans for Friday night?" is with a particular rising intonation, that indicates "I'm tired of hearing about your boyfriend, let's talk about something else." Note that if someone were to ask you about your usage of rising intonation in English and why you made use of it the way that you do, you probably would have no idea of what they are talking about: We are generally unaware of how we make use of our linguistic knowledge. The same holds true for bilinguals and how they make use of code-switching.

7.4 Conclusion

In conclusion, the fact that code-switching obeys general structural constraints and is used in linguistically abstract and rule-governed ways indicates that it is a sophisticated, linguistically significant use of language. It provides to bilinguals another way to express meaning in language.

Suggested Materials and Resources

Check out Bill Santiago's comical look at Spanglish in his book *Pardon my Spanglish* (2008).

Linguist Betty Bimer addresses concerns that the use of English in the USA is being threatened by the rise of minority languages, particularly Spanish. Bimer says that not only is English firmly established in America, no language has ever held as strong a position in the world as English does today (Bimer, n.d.).

The ground-breaking work on code-switching of Ana Celia Zentella (1997) discusses the complex linguistic processes that underlie code-switching.

CHAPTER 8

Are there Primitive Languages?

All languages meet the social and psychological needs of their speakers, are equally deserving of scientific study, and can provide us with valuable information about human nature and society.

David Crystal (2010, p. 6)

8.1 Introduction

It is commonly believed that there are languages which are "more primitive" than other languages. (The proponents of such a view unfailingly regard their own language as the more sophisticated language, and the one spoken by "other people" as the primitive language.) This may be understood in several ways: people may consider a language to be primitive if it does not have a written form, or if it is considered to have a small vocabulary and the ability to express only simple ideas, or maybe it is considered primitive if it is thought to "lack grammar": to allow words to occur in any order in a sentence. In this chapter, we will consider these three claims.

8.2 Written and Spoken Languages

It is natural for us as people who are educated in the written form of a language to consider that written form to be an essential part of the language. However, consider the fact that every human language is a spoken language (either using the vocal-auditory system or by being signed with the hands), whereas most of the world's languages do not have a written form. Anyone who attempts to learn a language which happens to not have a written form can confirm that these languages are as complex and expressive as any written language.

Significantly, all writing systems are based upon systems of spoken language which necessarily developed first. Historians believe that human language may have emerged at least half a million years ago; however, written language appeared fewer than 5,000 years ago (Uomini & Meyer, 2013).

8.2.1 Language ≠ Written Form

In fact, there is no inherent connection between a spoken language and its written form. For example, Persian (Farsi) is the main language of Iran, and is an Indo-European language. Persian is thus much closer genetically to English than it is to Arabic, which is a Semitic language, from a separate language family. However, due to the historical influence of Arabic speakers on the area of Persia (later called Iran), Persian is written in the Arabic alphabet.

Isssues around which script is chosen for a given language often have more to do with political, cultural, and social factors than with considerations of language structure. Azerbaijani, the main language of the country of Azerbaijan, is a Turkic language (a member of the Ural-Altaic language family, distinct from the Indo-European and Semitic families mentioned above). Although traditionally written in Arabic script, the language started to be written in the Cyrillic alphabet (the script used for Russian) when the area became part of the Soviet Union. Upon becoming an independent country in 1990, Azerbaijan adopted the Latin alphabet for representing the language. However, the language is the same, whether it is written in the Arabic, Cyrillic, or Latin alphabet. Therefore, whether a language happens to have a written form, and the particular written form that a language has, is completely independent of its linguistic structure, and has more to do with historical and social factors than linguistic ones.

8.3 Expression of Ideas in Different Languages

Languages may differ in the number of words they have; however, what gets counted as "a separate word" is not a simple issue. For example, in English, we have the word *small*, which can be used to modify a noun, as in *small children*. We also have the word *smaller*, which is the comparative form of this adjective, and the superlative form *smallest*. The question is: Do we count all three of these separate forms as three words, or as three separate forms of a single word? Depending on how we answer questions like this, we may come to very different conclusions about the number of words a given language has.

8.3.1 Building Words and Sentences in English and Turkish

This issue arises more dramatically in examining the words of many of the world's languages. English is regarded as an isolating language, which means that sentences are constructed from words, many of which carry only one meaning. For example, in English, we have the sentence below, comprised of 10 words:

(8.1)

   Are you one of those whom we could not Europeanize?

This sentence comes out as one word in Turkish, which is called an agglutinative language—a language which makes use of word-building processes to form very large and complex words from a single simple word:

(8.2)

   Avrupalılaştıramadıklarımızdanmısınız?

Let us break down this word to see how it is structured:

   Avrupa
   "Europe"
   ↓ *Avrupalı*
   "European"
   ↓ *Avrupalılaş*
   "become European"
   ↓ *Avrupalılaştır*
   "Europeanize" (command)

↓ *Avrupalılaştır**ama***

"I wish you could not Europeanize"

↓ *Avrupalılaştırama**dık***

"we could not Europeanize"

↓ *Avrupalılaştıramadık**lar***

"those whom could not Europeanize"

↓ *Avrupalılaştıramadıklar**ımız***

"those whom we could not Europeanize"

↓ *Avrupalılaştıramadıklarımız**dan***

"one of those whom we could not Europeanize"

↓ *Avrupalılaştıramadıklarımızdan**mı**?*

"Is s/he one of those whom we could not Europeanize?"

↓ *Avrupalılaştıramadıklarımızdan**mısın**?*

"Are you one of those whom we could not Europeanize?"

↓ *Avrupalılaştıramadıklarımızdanmıs**ınız**?*

"Are you (formal) one of those whom we could not Europeanize?"

However, notice what happens if an English speaker discovers that there is a concept for which there is no single word in English. English has the flexibility to create new words. This can happen by using two words that already exist in English and by combining them together. For example, when the New York pastry chef Dominique Ansel created a new pastry that was half donut, half croissant, he named it a *cronut* (Gopnik, 2014). We have other strategies for making new words in English—the word *unfriend* means "to remove someone from a list of friends or contacts on a social networking site." We had the word *befriend* already in English, meaning to make someone a friend. Since the prefix *un-* means to do the opposite of something, as in *untie my shoes*, we can use *un-* and *friend* to create a new word.

All human languages work this way; they all have the capacity to create new words by altering existing ones or coining new words.

8.3.2 Differences in Language Complexity

The claim that some languages have the ability to express only simple ideas is a myth. You may ask though, if you wanted to have a discussion about theoretical physics, would it be possible to do this in, for example, Arrernte, a Native Australian language which is spoken in and around Alice Springs in the Northern Territory (see Breen, 2001). The answer is that it is, given that the language has resources to introduce into its vocabulary new terms. This is exactly equivalent to a native speaker of Arrernte inquiring whether English is complex enough to be able to discuss all of the distinct ways in which a particular plant root might be altered in order to make it suitable for different medicinal purposes. Although it is possible that there has never been a conversation in English about this topic, speakers of English have the capacity to use language in a creative way and to talk about new concepts. All languages work this way.

I once attended a lecture on the topic of African American English Vernacular (AAEV), a dialect of English which we will discuss in the next chapter. The speaker greeted the audience and then proceeded to explain a complex analysis of the verbal system of AAEV, completely in AAEV. Many members of the audience had difficulty following the lecture, until the speaker stopped and said, "Well, I guess I've convinced you now that AAEV is a system in which complex theoretical ideas can be easily discussed." Touché.

However, this is not to say that languages cannot vary in the degree of convenience with which they describe certain things. For example, if I have two brothers who are older than me, how do I distinguish them from each other? I have to say something like *my oldest older brother*, versus *my second-oldest older brother*. In Chinese, the older of the two older brothers would be *da go* and the younger of the two older brothers would be *er ge*. Both Chinese and English can describe this meaning, but Chinese does so in a more economical manner.

Linguists have discovered that all languages have a system of sounds, words, and sentences that adequately communicates the content of the culture. As anyone who has studied a "primitive" language knows well, these languages are invariably complex in their grammatical structures. There seems to be no correlation between a particular structure of language and the technological level of a society or any other aspect of culture. This brings us to our third myth.

8.4 Do All Languages Have Grammar?

The English sentence *Kate ate a piece of cake* may be translated into Hungarian in several different ways, as shown below:

(8.3)

    a.   *Kati megevett egy szelet tortát.*
           Kate ate a piece of cake.

    b.   *Egy szelet tortát Kati evett meg.*
           A piece of cake Kate ate.   (emphasis on *Kate*)

    c.   *Kati egy szelet tortát evett meg.*
           Kate a piece of cake ate.   (emphasis on *cake*)

    d.   *Egy szelet tortát evett meg Kati.*
           A piece of cake ate Kate.   (emphasis on number, only
                                                  one piece)

    e.   *Megevett egy szelet tortát Kati.*
           Ate a piece of cake Kate.   (emphasis on completeness
                                                  of action)

    f.   *Megevett Kati egy szelet tortát.*
           Ate Kate a piece of cake.   (emphasis on finished
                                                  action)

We may be tempted to say that Hungarian is a "free word-order language," whereas English is a "fixed word-order language." However, there are several problems with dividing up languages into these two types.

8.4.1 No Language has Free Word Order

First of all, there has never been attested a human language which allows the words of the sentence to appear in any order. There are generalizations about the possible permutations that different languages exhibit, but all languages observe restrictions on the order in which words may appear. For example, although in Hungarian it is possible to have all of the different word orders shown above, the following word orders are **not** possible:

(8.4)

    a.   *Egy szelet Kati megevett tortat.*
          A piece of Kate ate cake

    b.   *Szelet megevett tortat Kati egy.*
          Piece of ate cake Kate a

All human languages show restrictions on what is possible in the structure of a sentence.

It is also important to note that it is not the case that using different word orders results in identical meanings for sentences. Notice that the emphasis that is given to different parts of the sentence depends on where those words occur in the sentence in Hungarian, as shown by the meanings in parentheses.

This is also true for English. Although the neutral version of a sentence is *I could watch Project Runway all day long*, we may emphasize *Project Runway* by moving it to the front of the sentence, to get *Project Runway, I could watch all day long.* Notice that the meaning is now something like, "In contrast to Anthony Bourdain: No Reservations, which I can really only watch for about three hours in a row max, Project Runway is something that I could devote a whole twelve hours to."

However, if we tried to change the sentence *I could watch Project Runway all day long* by moving the last word to the front of the sentence, we would get *Long, I could watch Project Runway all day*, which does not sound like a natural sentence of English (unless you are addressing someone named Long, and you are telling them that you could watch *Project Runway* all day. In this case, the meaning of the sentence changes and so it is no longer the same sentence.)

8.4.2 Click Consonants

The opinion that people may hold of a particular property of a language is not related to any objective linguistic measure. For example, let us say that I think that Spanish is a beautiful, romantic language. It is fine for me to hold this belief, but it is just a belief. It cannot be scientifically proven that Spanish is a beautiful, romantic language, since what is considered beautiful and romantic is not able to be measured objectively.

Many people consider the "click" sounds found in certain languages of southern and east Africa, such as Zulu, Hadza, and Dahalo, to be exotic sounds, and they wonder how the speakers of these languages can produce such unusual sounds. Click sounds are produced with two points of contact in the mouth, one forward and one at the back. The pocket of air enclosed between these points of contact is created by an intake of air, and the forward point of closure is released, producing the click. The Xhosa language, spoken in South Africa, has 18 distinct click sounds (see Jessen & Roux, 2002).

Languages with click sounds have been ridiculed because these sounds seem to be so distinctly different from the sounds produced in other languages. On the other hand, others have argued that these click sounds support the claim that these languages are related to "the original human language."

8.4.2.1 English Click Consonants

Notice that, although these sounds seem to be "exotic" from the point of view of English, several of these are used in English:

(8.5) Click Consonants in English

a. *tsk tsk* (dental click)	This is used as an expression of dismay or disagreement. The tongue touches the back of the teeth as air is sucked into the mouth.
b. *clip-clop*	This is the sound children make with their tongue to imitate a horse trotting; this is an alveopalatal click—the tongue is farther back in the mouth than when producing the *tsk tsk* click.
c. *tchick*	This sound is made by lifting the sides of the tongue upwards to touch the roof of the mouth.

d. air kiss	The sound of an "air kiss" is made by pursing the lips together and inhaling air and then letting the air out by opening the lips. This is called a bilabial click.

Speakers of English, it turns out, also use clicks for a previously overlooked purpose: as a form of verbal punctuation in between thoughts or phrases. Melissa Wright (2011) analyzes click sounds in six large sets of recorded English conversations. She found that speakers used clicks frequently to signal that they were ending one stretch of conversation and shifting to a new one. For example, a speaker might say, "Yeah, that was a great game," produce a click, then say, "The reason I'm calling is to invite you to dinner tomorrow."

This pattern, which occurs for both British and American speakers, suggests that clicks have a meaning similar to saying *anyway* or *so*. That is, clicks provide us with a phonetic resource to organize conversations and communicate our intentions to listeners. This finding had previously eluded linguists, whose research often focuses on words and sentences in isolation. Wright was able to uncover the new pattern because she analyzed clicks in the context of complete conversations, suggesting that this method is important in understanding overlooked linguistic phenomena.

The linguistic analysis of these consonant sounds includes a description of how they are physically produced and how they function in the languages that systematically have them. The way in which people choose to view the production of such sounds has more to do with opinions that people hold of the speakers of the language than with anything objectively linguistic. This is generally true for claims that certain languages are "primitive"; this is more descriptive of the perspective that someone may have on a particular culture than on anything remotely linguistically objective.

8.5 Conclusion

All human languages share far more in common than they differ. All attested languages have three major components: a sound system, a vocabulary, and a system of grammar. All languages have unlimited resources for the expression of thought and emotion.

All human languages are complex. It does not matter where speakers live or what kind of lifestyle they have, all languages have internal structures which are systematically ordered by rules. In conclusion, there is no such thing as a primitive language.

Suggested Materials and Resources

There is recent debate over the claim that all languages exhibit recursion. Daniel Everett has argued that Pirahã, a native language of Brazil, in fact lacks recursion (Everett, 2005). For vigorous discussion of this claim, see Nevins, Pesetsky, & Rodrigues (2009a), Everett (2009), Nevins, Pesetsky & Rodrigues (2009b), and Sauerland (2010).

CHAPTER 9

Non-Standard Dialects

9.1 Introduction

When we first meet someone, we form an impression of that person on the basis of many things, for example, how she is dressed, how she is standing, her hairstyle, her height. A significant part of our evaluation of someone includes the manner in which the person speaks: If they sound like they come from Texas, or from Russia, or from Southern California, we are likely to evaluate the person differently.

Sociolinguistics is the area of linguistics that is interested in understanding the variation that occurs within language: Why do different groups of speakers speak in distinct ways? What are the historical reasons for language variation? How can we describe the varieties that occur across different groups? We will see that gender, class, geographical region, and ethnicity can all play a role in how people speak.

A professor of mine at the University of Massachusetts was originally from a small city in Mississippi. When he began his graduate studies at the University of Chicago, he quickly learned that when he spoke in his native variety of English, people had a reaction of either finding it very humorous, or thinking that he could not possibly know what he was talking about. When he would express the same ideas in a northern variety of English, all of a sudden things changed—he was taken more seriously as a thinker. He decided to try to completely eradicate any traces of his southern accent. It was not until years later, when he happened to take a course with a professor who was originally from Texas, and had maintained his native accent, that he started to question his decision. The first reaction of the class to the professor speaking in the Texas variety of English was, "This must be a joke; he can't be serious." But as he continued, it took little time for the students to adjust to his style of speech.

The acknowledgment that features of our language depend on the language group(s) that we belong to leads us to the interesting question of what is a dialect. In particular, we might wonder what the difference is between a language and a dialect. Linguists define the distinction between a language and a dialect as being determined by mutual intelligibility: If two speakers can understand each other, then they are speaking the same language although they may be speaking two different dialects. If they cannot understand each other, they are speaking different languages.

However, the way in which the terms *language* and *dialect* are commonly used is often distinct from this linguistic definition. For example, Norwegian and Danish are mutually intelligible, and yet they are considered to be two separate languages. On the other hand, there are many languages spoken in China which are not mutually intelligible, but which are referred to as different dialects of Chinese. It is also the case that many dialects of what we call "English" are not mutually intelligible. If you watch the film *Trainspotting* and you are not familiar with Scottish English, you may need to make use of the captions.

The linguist Max Weinreich famously came to the conclusion that, "A language is a dialect with an army and a navy." In other words, the way in which the terms *language* and *dialect* are commonly used often has more to do with national boundaries and political and social factors, than with the linguistic concept of mutual intelligibility. Linguists acknowledge that the common usage of these terms is independent of linguistic factors, while maintaining the definition based on mutual intelligibility for linguistic discussions of language.

If someone were to ask you, "Do you speak a dialect?", think of what your reaction would be. You may conclude that you do not speak a dialect, since what you speak is "just English." However, consider this: there is no form of any language which is outside of linguistic description. In other words, every form of every language has associated with it characteristics that distinguish it from all of the other ways of speaking the language, and thus, everyone who speaks a language in fact necessarily speaks a dialect (a variety) of that language. The reason that many people say that they do not speak a dialect is that the term *dialect* is stigmatized. Speakers often consider *variety* to be more neutral than *dialect*, although linguists use these terms interchangeably to refer to a particular form of a language.

9.2 Register

Note what your reaction would be if the first paragraph of this chapter had begun as follows:

> First time you meet up with someone new, you're gonna get a vibe off a whole lotta things—like, how are they dressin', how are they presentin', their style ... if you run into someone with a really thick Texas twang, or a Russian accent or someone who you know they're from Southern Calie, you get a real different picture in your mind of who you're talkin' to.

instead of:

> When we first meet someone, we form an impression of that person on the basis of many things, for example, how she is dressed, how she is standing, her hairstyle, her height. A significant part of our evaluation of someone includes the manner in which the person speaks: If they sound like they come from Texas, or from Russia, or from Southern California, we are likely to evaluate the person differently.

You would probably be a bit surprised to read a book for a college course written in this style, although you would understand perfectly the meaning. The reason for your surprise is that the changed paragraph is written in an informal style associated with casual spoken English. In fact, most speakers of English (or any language) have at least several different forms of the language that they use depending on the context, even though they might not be aware of this. Whether your language is written or spoken, whether you are giving an address to the Nobel Prize committee or you are sitting at the kitchen table with your mom, you are likely to express what may be the same ideas in different ways. These distinctions that each individual has in the forms of a given language are what are called registers.

A register is thus different from a dialect (or variety) in that it is defined at the level of the individual, as opposed to the level of the group. Of course, many speakers of a language speak several registers, as well as different dialects. For example, if you grew up in a small town in Georgia, you would probably be a native speaker of a variety of Southern English (a dialect). Within this dialect, you would possess different registers—formal or informal—which you would utilize in different language contexts. You would probably also speak a variety of English which many people call Standard American English, and within this dialect you would possess several registers as well.

9.3 Standard and Non-Standard English

The key concept in understanding variation in dialects is to realize that dialects differ from each other in exactly the same way that different languages differ from each other. There are no predictable linguistic differences across different languages that do not also distinguish standard from non-standard dialects. A linguistic feature that may be stigmatized in a particular dialect of a language may be considered part of the standard language in another dialect.

For example, Standard American English and Standard British English (sometimes called Received Pronunciation, or RP) differ with respect to several properties, illustrated here:

Standard American	Standard British
I've *gotten* over that problem.	I've *got* over that problem.
She *dove* into the water.	She *dived* into the water.
I might have done *it*.	I might have done.
The committee *is* meeting today.	The committee *are* meeting today.
Bill is in *the hospital*.	Bill is in *hospital*.

From the point of view of language variation, this is expected, since these are distinct regional dialects of English; there is no reason to think that because they are both standard dialects of English, they will share all of their linguistic features.

9.3.1 Pronunciation of /r/

A major distinction between different varieties of English is in how the /r/ sound is pronounced after vowels. William Labov pioneered the modern study of sociolinguistics by performing an experiment in 1966 that examined how speakers pronounce words with this sound, such as *fourth* and *floor*. In some dialects of American English the /r/ sound is pronounced in these words, and in other dialects it is not.

Labov was interested in understanding if the pronunciation of /r/ in the English spoken in New York City varied according to the social class of the speaker. He hypothesized that in New York City English, it is more prestigious to pronounce the /r/ sound and less prestigious to leave it out. He investigated this claim by visiting three department stores that vary according to social class: Saks Fifth Avenue (upper class), Macy's (middle class), and S. Klein (working class). In each store, he asked a sales attendant where an item that he knew to be on the fourth floor was located, thereby eliciting the answer *The fourth floor*. Labov found that the sales assistants from Saks Fifth Avenue pronounced the /r/ sound most frequently, showing that the prestigious form in New York was to pronounce the /r/. Those from Macy's showed variation in its pronunciation, and those from Klein's used it least, pronouncing *floor* as "flaw."

Interestingly, the correlation of the pronunciation of /r/ after vowels in American English with a higher-class form of the language does not hold in other American dialects of English. If you are familiar with the Boston dialect of English, you will know that the lack of the pronunciation of /r/ is present in working-class dialects, as illustrated in the movie *Good Will Hunting*. However, /r/-less pronunciation is also common in the so-called Boston Brahmin dialect, associated with the well-educated, wealthy elite of Boston, made famous by the speech of the Kennedy family.

So, within American English, /r/-less pronunciation after vowels may be associated with different classes of speech. It is also the case that American and British English differ in this way: in the English of Reading, England, pronouncing the /r/ sound after vowels is associated with working-class speech, while less pronunciation of /r/ is associated with middle-class speech, and the lack of /r/ after vowels is associated with educated, upper-class speech. The English of Reading, England presents essentially the mirror image of New York City English with respect to the status associated with the pronunciation of /r/ after vowels.

9.4 African-American English Vernacular

In the remainder of this chapter, I will discuss a dialect of English known as African-American English Vernacular (AAEV). In examining the features of this non-standard dialect, we will see that the rules and patterns that are followed in this form of English are as regular and abstract as any form of English.

However, before we begin to investigate properties of AAEV, a word about the name of this dialect is required. The name seems to draw a correlation between race and dialect. However, this is oversimplifying, since any person, of any color or ethnic background, will necessarily learn the language that is spoken around them as they are growing up. For example, an ethnically Japanese baby who is raised hearing AAEV will speak AAEV. A child who happens to be of African descent who does not hear AAEV growing up, but instead hears a dialect of Tokyo Japanese, will have the dialect of Tokyo Japanese that they are exposed to. There is no inherent correlation between race or ethnicity and a particular form of language.

9.4.1 Grammatical Patterns of AAEV
9.4.1.1 Null *be*
One of the interesting features of AAEV sentences is that they may occur with a null form of the verb *be*. For example, one may say *She tall*, whereas in the standard form of American English, one would say *She is tall*. If you are a monolingual speaker of standard English,

your initial reaction to a sentence such as this might be, "But where's the verb? You can't have a sentence without a verb—something is missing here!"

However, linguists have noted that there are many languages in the world which have this same structure, such as Modern Hebrew, Russian, and Swedish. Examples from Modern Hebrew are provided in (9.1):

(9.1) Modern Hebrew:

    a.   *Rina*   *talmida.*
           Rina   student
       "Rina is a student."

    b.   *Rina*   *xaxama.*
           Rina   intelligent
       "Rina is intelligent."

    c.   *Rina*   *ba*   *bayit.*
           Rina   at   home
       "Rina is at home."

The literal translation of the sentence *Rina is intelligent* is "Rina intelligent" in Hebrew. It is interesting to note that no one questions how Hebrew or Russian or Swedish can have sentences without verbs or complains about these examples, since, just as in AAEV, this is the only verb that can appear null. This shows that it is crucial for linguists to examine non-standard varieties of language just as they would different languages.

9.4.1.2 Habitual Invariant *be*

Another interesting construction of AAEV is habitual invariant *be*; the usage of the verb *be* in sentences such as (9.2):

(9.2)

    They be talking all the time.

Notice that there is a particular interpretation that is associated with this usage of the verb *be*—it refers to something that happens regularly, habitually. Therefore, it is not possible to say in AAEV something like (9.3):

(9.3)

   *They be answering the door right now.

The verbal system of AAEV in this sense is thus more complex than that of Standard English, since in order to express habitual meaning, there is no distinct verb form in Standard English—it is expressed instead by phrases like *usually* or *all the time*.

9.4.1.3 Intensive *steady*

AAEV shows another verbal distinction not present in Standard English, exemplified in the following sentence:

(9.4)

   He be steady runnin'.

Since we have invariant *be* here, we know that the meaning is habitual, describing an action that takes place regularly. The meaning that *steady* adds to this construction is that the running takes place in an intensive, steady manner. As we would expect, there are many languages around the world that have a distinct form of the intensive meaning of the verb, and so this property of AAEV is not unique.

9.4.1.4 Present Relevance *bin* Form

AAEV has sentences such as the following:

(9.5)

   He bin runnin'.

The meaning of this is expressed in Standard English as *He has been running*, with the use of the present perfect form of the verb. The interpretation is that there is present relevance to the expression. In other words, if one were to say *He bin runnin'* in AAEV, it would be understood as something like, "Given how he looks right now, it makes sense to say that he has been engaged in the act of running."

9.4.1.5 Stressed *bin* Form

A distinct form of *bin* occurs in AAEV, in a sentence such as:

(9.6)

He <u>bin</u> runnin'.

Notice that this sentence is pronounced with stress on the word *bin* and is thus distinct from the sentence *He bin runnin'* where there is no stress on the word *bin*. The meaning of this sentence is expressed in Standard English as, "He started running in the past and he is still running right now." Notice that these distinctions are sometimes very important in carrying different meanings: *She bin married* means that she was married in the past, but may not be right now, whereas *She <u>bin</u> married* means that she got married and she is now married.

9.4.1.6 Empty *it*

In AAEV, it is possible to find sentences such as the following:

(9.7)

It was a party last night.

In Standard English, this sentence would be:

(9.8)

There was a party last night.

The use of the subject *it* without any meaning can be found in the following Standard English sentence:

(9.9)

It is raining.

Notice that it is not surprising that we see variation in the use of these empty subjects in different dialects of English, since different languages also make use of different structures with respect to these sentences. We can see this in the following Spanish sentences:

(9.10)

> *Esta*   *lloviendo.*
> is   raining
> "It is raining."

(9.11)

> *Hay*   *cinco*   *perros*   *en*   *la*   *habitacion.*
> There are   five   dogs   in   the   room
> "There are five dogs in the room."

In the weather construction in Spanish, there is no need to include a subject; in fact, including one would be impossible:

(9.12)

> **El*   *esta*   *lloviendo.*
> It   is   raining.

However, in the *there* construction, we have a distinct form *hay* that is utilized. This indicates that the way in which different languages treat these constructions differs, and thus it is not surprising that AAEV shows variation in this respect.

9.4.1.7 Negative Structures in AAEV

AAEV shows very interesting properties with respect to negation. This dialect has multiple negation and negative inversion, as do many other non-standard dialects of American English.

Double Negatives

In AAEV, it is possible to say:

(9.13)

> I ain't got no time for that.

In Standard American English (SAE), one would say *I don't have any time for that*. Recall from Chapter 1 that it is expected that, in some dialects of English, we would find double negative structures, since they are quite common across the languages of the world.

Negative Inversion

We find sentences such as the following in AAEV:

(9.14)

Don't nobody know about that.

The SAE version of the sentence would be *Nobody knows about that*. Notice that the AAEV sentence thus displays double negation, as in (9.15):

(9.15)

Nobody don't know about that.

In addition, it shows inversion of the word *don't*. Recall that this process of moving the auxiliary verb to the front of the sentence is a pattern that we have discussed in English questions, such as:

(9.16)

   a.   Mary will come to the party.
   b.   Will Mary come to the party?

Interestingly, this process in AAEV is subject to the same generalizations and constraints that we observed in our earlier discussion about the Rule of Question Formation in English. For example, recall that in question formation it is necessary to move the first of a sequence of auxiliary verbs, giving us the contrast between the following sentences:

(9.17)

   a.   Mary will have come to the party by 5:00.
   b.   *Have Mary will come to the party by 5:00?
   c.   Will Mary have come to the party by 5:00?

If the way in which negative inversion takes place in AAEV is the same as the way in which question formation operates in SAE, then we expect to find the same data in this dialect, as is shown by the following:

(9.18)

   a.   Nobody won't be comin' to no party if you don't fix things up.

   b.   Won't nobody be comin' to no party if you don't fix things up.

   c.   *Be nobody won't comin' to no party if you don't fix things up.

Notice that we have a remnant of negative inversion in SAE, involving negative words such as *never*, as in:

(9.19)

Never have I seen such a beautiful sight.

Although this sounds somewhat formal and stilted in spoken English, if we found this in a formal text we would not be too surprised. This indicates that the process of inverting the auxiliary verb when negation is present is a pattern that is reflected in older patterns of English and remains to some extent in contemporary formal registers of SAE, as well as being productive in AAEV. (Notice the different reactions that saying *Won't nobody be comin' to the party tonight if you don't fix things up* will elicit, as opposed to the structurally very similar *Never have I seen such a beautiful sight.*)

9.4.2 The Sound Patterns of AAEV

Just as AAEV has distinctive sentence patterns, it also shows unique patterns in its phonology, its sound system.

9.4.2.1 Non-Word-Initial *th*

In AAEV, the word *bath* is often pronounced as /baf/, and the word *with* as /wif/. It seems that the /th/ sound in SAE is replaced with the /f/ sound in AAEV. However, there are restrictions on where this process takes place. Given the following examples, what is the generalization?

(9.20)

bath	/baf/
with	/wif/
think	*/fink/
month	/monf/
Bethlehem	/Beflehem/
theory	*/feory/
myth	/myf/

So, speakers will say /monf/, /Beflehem/, and /myf/, but not, */fink/ or */feory/. The generalization is that /f/ is pronounced when it occurs in a position in the word that is not initial.

There are many sound processes in language which are restricted according to position in the word. For example, in English, although we have the sound /ng/ as in *sing*, we do not find this sound at the beginning of a word. Thus, we would not expect to find a word such as **ngall*, although we might find a word in English that sounds like *nall*, or *gall*. This is not true for all languages; in Rapanui, Bambara, and Ngiyambaa, we do find word initial /ng/ sounds, as we can see in the name of the language Ngiyambaa.

Likewise, in AAEV, we find non-word initial instances of the "hard th" sound, as in *smooth*, *mother*, and *bathe*, pronounced as /smoov/, /mover/, and /bave/. However, as expected we do not find the word *this*, where the sound occurs at the beginning of the word, pronounced as */vis/, or *there* pronounced as */vere/. Instead, in this position, the word may be pronounced with a /d/ sound, like /dis/ and /dere/.

9.4.2.2 Final Consonant Deletion

AAEV shows deletion of consonants in word-final position, such as /tes/ for *test*, /des/ for *desk*. However, notice that speakers of AAEV do not pronounce a word such as *heat* as */hea/ or a word such as *lick* as */li/. The final consonant sound of a word is deleted only if there is a series of consonants at the end: /st/ in *test*, /sk/ in *desk*. Another restriction that this process shows is that the two sounds have to both be voiced (produced with vibration in the vocal chords, as in /b/, /z/, or /d/) or both be unvoiced (produced without vibration in the vocal chords, as in /p/, /s/, /t/). So when we have a word with a sequence of consonants at the end, there can only be final consonant deletion if the two sounds are matched with respect to voicing; therefore, the word, *sharp* is not pronounced as */shar/ in AAEV, since the sound /r/ is voiced, and the sound /p/ is unvoiced.

9.5 Conclusion

To summarize this chapter, all human beings speak a language, and all speakers of a language speak a dialect (or dialects) of that language; a dialect is just a particular variety of a language. The differences between a standard and non-standard variety of the language are not predictable, and non-standard varieties, such as African-American English Vernacular, are just as logical and rule-based as standard forms of the language. The most skilled language users are not those who avoid using different dialects; they are those who master the use of different varieties of language to achieve different communicative goals.

Suggested Materials and Resources

For discussion of the structure of AAEV, see Pullum (1999), Green (2002), Rickford (2002), Rickford & National Council of Teachers of English (2013), and Lanehart (2015).

Jamila Lyiscott is a tri-tongued orator, and in her powerful spoken-word essay *Broken English* (Lyiscott, 2014), she celebrates the three distinct dialects of English she speaks with her friends, in the classroom, and with her parents.

References

Abugaber-Bowman, D. (2014). *New experimental methods in language learning research* [YouTube lecture]. GatesCambridge. Retrieved from https://www.youtube.com/watch?v=ms7023jmTIk

Ambridge, B., & Rowland, C. F. (2013). Experimental methods in studying child language acquisition. *WIREs Cognitive Science, 4*(2), 149–168 https://doi.org/10.1002/wcs.1215

Anderson, S. (2006). *Doctor Dolittle's delusion*. New Haven, CT: Yale University Press.

Arias, R., & Lakshmanan, U. (2005). Code-switching in a SpanishEnglish bilingual child: A communication reference. In J. Cohen, K. T. McAlister, K. Rolstad, & J. MacSwan (Eds.) *Proceedings of the International Symposium on Bilingualism* (pp. 94–109). Somerville, MA: Cascadilla Press.

Atkinson, R., Bem, D. J., Smith, E., Renner, M., & Atkinson, R. C. (1993). *Introduction to psychology*. Fort Worth, TX: Harcourt Brace Jovanovich.

Babyonyshev, M., & Brun, D. (2004). The acquisition of perfective and imperfective passive constructions in Russian. *University of Pennsylvania Working Papers in Linguistics, 10*(1:3). Retrieved from https://repository.upenn.edu/pwpl/vol10/iss1/3

Bellows, A. (2008). *Clever Hans the math horse*. Retrieved from www.damninteresting.com/clever-hans-the-math-horse/

Bellugi, U. (1967). The acquisition of negation (Doctoral dissertation). Harvard University, Cambridge, MA.

Benedict, H. (1979). Early lexical development: Comprehension and production. *Journal of Child Language, 6*, 183–200.

Berger, M. (2008). Measurement of vowel nasalization by multi-dimensional acoustic analysis. *Working Papers in the Language Sciences at the University of Rochester*. Winter 2008, 4.1.

Berk-Seligson, S. (1986). Linguistic constraints on intrasentential code-switching: A study of Spanish/Hebrew bilingualism. *Language in Society, 15*(3), 313–348. https://doi.org/10.1017/S0047404500011799

Berwick, R., & Chomsky, N. (2011). The biolinguistic program: The current state of its evolution and development. In A. M. Di Sciullo & C. Boeckx (Eds.) *The biolinguistic enterprise: New perspectives on the evolution and nature of the human language faculty* (pp. 19–41). Oxford: Oxford University Press.

Bimer, B. (n.d.) *Habla español? Does Spanish threaten American English?* Retrieved from www.pbs.org/speak/seatosea/americanvarieties/spanglish/threat/ (accessed at itre.cis.upenn.edu on 3 July 2017).

Bley-Vroman, R. W., Felix, S. W., & Ioup, G. L. (1988). The accessibility of universal grammar in adult language learning. *Second Language Research, 4*(1), 1–32. https://doi.org/10.1177/026765838800400101

Boylan, C., Trueswell, J. C., & Thompson-Schill, S. L. (2017, June). Relational vs. attributive interpretation of nominal compounds differentially engages angular gyrus and anterior temporal lobe. *Brain & Language, 169*, 8–21. https://doi.org/10.1016/j.bandl.2017.01.008

Breen, G. (2001). The wonders of Arandic phonology. In J. Simpson, D. Nash, M. Laughren, P. Austin, & B. Alpher (Eds.) *Forty years on: Ken Hale and Australian languages* (pp. 45–69). Canberra: Pacific Linguistics, Australian National University.

Broselow, E., & Finer, D. (1991). Parameter setting in second language phonology and syntax. *Second Language Research, 7*(1), 35–59. https://doi.org/10.1177/026765839100700102

Brown, R. (1973). *A first language: The early stages*. Cambridge, MA: Harvard University Press. https://doi.org/10.4159/harvard.9780674732469

Brown, R., & Hanlon, C. (1970). Derivational complexity and order of acquisition in child speech. In J.R. Hayes (Ed.), *Cognition and the development of language* (pp. 11–53). New York: Wiley.

Caro, T .M., & Hauser, M.D. (1992). Is there teaching in nonhuman animals? *The Quarterly Review of Biology, 67*(2), 151–174. https://doi.org/10.1086/417553

Chaucer, G. (1987). *Riverside Chaucer* (3rd edn, ed. L. Benson). New York: Houghton Mifflin.

Chimpanzee Sanctuary Northwest. (2010). *Chimpanzee vocalizations* [YouTube presentation]. Retrieved from www.youtube.com/watch?v=OQFOi5Whlzk

Chomsky, N. (1959). [Review of the book *Verbal Behavior*, by B. F. Skinner]. *Language, 35*(1), 26–58. https://doi.org/10.2307/411334

Chomsky, N. (1965). *Aspects of the theory of syntax*. Cambridge, MA: MIT Press.

Chomsky, N. (1967). The formal nature of language. In E. H. Lenneberg (Ed.), *Biological foundations of language* (pp.397–442). New York: Wiley and Sons.

Chomsky, N. (1971). The case against B. F. Skinner. *New York Review of Books*, December 30. Retrieved from https://www.nybooks.com/articles/1971/12/30/the-case-against-bf-skinner/

Chomsky, N. (1972). *Language and mind*. New York: Harcourt Brace Jovanovich.

Chomsky, N. (1991). Linguistics and cognitive science: Problems and mysteries. In A. Kasher (Ed.), *The Chomskyan Turn* (pp. 26–53). Oxford: Basil Blackwell.

Comrie, B., Matthews, S., & Polinksy M. (Eds). (2003). *The atlas of languages: The origin and development of languages throughout the world.* New York: Checkmark Books.

Crago, M. B., & Gopnik, M. (1994). From families to phenotypes: Theoretical and clinical implications of research into the genetic basis of specific language impairment. In R. Watkins & M. Rice (Eds.), *Specific language impairments in children* (pp. 35–51). Baltimore, MD: Paul H Brookes.

Crain, S., & Nakamaya, M. (1987). Structure dependence in grammar formation. *Language, 63*(3), 522–543.

Crystal, D. (2010). *The Cambridge encyclopedia of language.* Cambridge: Cambridge University Press.

Curtiss, S. (1978). *Genie: A psycholinguistic study of a modern-day "Wild Child".* Boston, MA: Academic Press.

Curtiss, S. (1988). Abnormal language acquisition and grammar: evidence for the modularity of language. In L. Hyman & C. Li (Eds.), *Language, speech and mind: Studies in honour of Victoria A. Fromkin* (pp. 81–102). London and New York: Routledge.

Curtiss, S. (1989a). The independence and task-specificity of language. In M. Bornstein & J. Bruner (Eds.), *Interaction in human development* (pp. 105–138). Hillsdale, NJ: Erlbaum.

Curtiss, S. (1989b). Abnormal Language Acquisition and the Modularity of Language. In F. Newmeyer (Ed.), *Linguistics: The Cambridge survey.* Cambridge: Cambridge University Press.

Degraff, M. (2005). Linguists' most dangerous myth: The fallacy of Creole Exceptionalism. *Language in Society, 34*(4), 533–591. https://doi.org/10.1017/S0047404505050207

De Houwer, A. (1990). *The acquisition of two languages from birth: A case study.* Cambridge: Cambridge University Press. https://doi.org/10.1017/CBO9780511519789

Déprez, V., & Pierce, A. (1993). Negation and functional projections in early grammar. *Linguistic Inquiry, 24*(1), 25–67.

Di Sciullo, A., Muysken, P., & Singh, R. (1986). Government and code-mixing. *Journal of Linguistics, 22*(1), 1–24.

Dowling, J. (2017). *Creating mind: How the brain works* (Rev. ed.). New York: W.W. Norton and Company.

Duffield, N., Matsuo, A., & Roberts, L. (2007). Acceptable ungrammaticality in sentence matching. *Second Language Research, 23*(2), 155–178. https://doi.org/10.1177/0267658307076544

Duffield, N., White, L., Bruhn de Garavito, J., & Montrul, S. (2002). Clitic placement in L2 French: Evidence from sentence matching. *Journal of Linguistics, 38*(3), 487–525. https://doi.org/10.1017/S0022226702001688

Van Dulm, O. (2006). Structural aspects of English–Afrikaans intrasentential code-switching. *Southern African Linguistics and Applied Language Studies, 24*(1), 57–69. https://doi.org/10.2989/16073610609486406

Van Dulm, O. (2007). The grammar of English–Afrikaans code switching: a feature checking account (PhD dissertation). LOT, Netherlands. Retrieved from www.lotpublications.nl/publish/articles/002423/bookpart.pdf.

Dutcher, N. (1998). Eritrea: Developing a programme of multilingual education. In J. Cenoz & F. Genesee (Eds.), *Beyond bilingualism: Multilinguals and multilingual education* (pp. 259–269). Clevedon, UK: Multilingual Matters.

Edwards, S. (2005). Fluent aphasia. Cambridge: Cambridge University Press.

Eubank, L. (1993/94). On the transfer of parametric values in L2 development. *Language Acquisition, 3*(3), 183–208. https://doi.org/10.1207/s15327817la0303_1

Everett, D. L. (2005). Cultural constraints on grammar and cognition in Pirahã: Another look at the design features of human language. *Current Anthropology, 46*(4), 621–646. https://doi.org/10.1086/431525

Everett, D. L. (2009). Pirahã culture and grammar: A response to some criticisms. *Language, 85*(2), 405–442. https://doi.org/10.1353/lan.0.0104

Fantini, A. E. (1985). *Language acquisition of a bilingual child: A sociolinguistic perspective (to age ten)*. Clevedon, UK: Multilingual Matters.

Fernald, A., Taeschner, T., Dunn, J., Papousek, M., De Boysson-Bardies, B., & Fukui, I. (1989). A cross-language study of prosodic modifications in mothers' and fathers' speech to preverbal infants. *Journal of Child Language, 16*(3), 477–501. https://doi.org/10.1017/S0305000900010679

Finegan, E. (2005). What is "correct" language?: Prescriptivism vs. descriptivism. In *Do you speak American?*, PBS South Florida, MacNeil/Lehrer Productions. https://www.pbs.org/speak/speech/correct/prescriptivism/

fistofblog. (2008). *Star Wars according to a three-year old* [YouTube clip]. Retrieved from www.youtube.com/watch?v=EBM854BTGLo

Fitch, W. T., de Boer, B., Mathur, N., & Ghanzanfar, A. (2016, December 9). Monkey vocal tracts are speech ready. *Science Advances, 2*(12), e1600723. https://doi.org/10.1126/sciadv.1600723

Floccia, C., Christophe, A., & Bertoncini, J. (1997). High-amplitude sucking and newborns: The quest for underlying mechanisms. *Journal of Experimental Child Psychology, 64*(2), 175–198. https://doi.org/10.1006/jecp.1996.2349

Flynn, S., & Martohardjono, G. (1995). Toward theory-driven language pedagogy. In F. Eckman, D. Highland, P. Lee, J. Mileham, & R. Weber (Eds.), *Second language acquisition theory and pedagogy* (pp. 45–59). Hove, UK: Erlbaum.

Fought, J. (2005). Barring the gates of language. In *Do you speak American?* Macneil/Lehrer Productions. Retrieved from www.pbs.org/speak/speech/correct/gatekeeping/summary/

von Frisch, K. (1927). *Aus dem Leben der Bienen*. Berlin: Springer Verlag. Translated and published as: *The dancing bees: An account of the life and senses of the honey bee*. New York: Harvest Books (1953).

von Frisch, K. (1967). *The dance language and orientation of bees*. Cambridge, MA: Harvard University Press.

von Frisch, K. (1973). *Decoding the Language of the Bee* [Nobel Lecture, 12 December 1973]. Retrieved from www.nobelprize.org/nobel_prizes/medicine/laureates/1973/frisch-lecture.html

Fromkin, V., Rodman, R., & Hyams, N. (2014). *An introduction to language*. Boston, MA: Wadsworth.

Gair, J.W., & Martohardjono, G. (1993). Apparent UG inaccessibility in second language acquisition: Misapplied principles or principled misapplications? In F. R. Eckman (Ed.), *Confluence: Linguistics, L2 acquisition and speech pathology* (pp. 79–103). Amsterdam: John Benjamins.

Gondry, M. (2013). *Is the man who is tall happy?* [Documentary film]. France: Partizan Films.

Gopnik, A. B. (2014, November 3). Bakeoff: What is happening to our pastry? *New Yorker*. Retrieved from https://www.newyorker.com/magazine/2014/11/03/bakeoff

Gopnik, M. (1994). Impairments of tense in a familial language disorder. *Journal of Neurolinguistics, 8*(2), 109–133. https://doi.org/10.1016/0911-6044(94)90020-5

Gopnik, M., & Crago, M. B. (1991, April). Familial Aggregation of a Developmental Language Disorder. *Cognition, 39*(1), 1–50. https://doi.org/10.1016/0010-0277(91)90058-C

Green, L. (2002). *African American English: A linguistic introduction*. Cambridge: Cambridge University Press. https://doi.org/10.1017/CBO9780511800306

Greiser, D. L., & Kuhl, P.K. (1988). Maternal speech to infants in a tonal language: Support for universal prosodic features in motherese. *Developmental Psychology, 24*(1), 14–20. https://dx.doi.org/10.1037/0012-1649.24.1.14

Guenole, M. (2013). *Siamang duet vs Gibbon: Battle* [YouTube clip]. Retrieved from www.youtube.com/watch?v=AkLLnvj0F-Q

Guitar, B. (2013). *Stuttering: An integrated approach to its nature and treatment*. Baltimore, MD: Lippincott Williams and Wilkins.

Haegeman, L. (2006). *Thinking syntactically. A Guide to argumentation and analysis*. Oxford: Blackwell Publishing.

Hauser, M. D., Chomsky, N., & Fitch, T. W. (2002, November 22). The faculty of language: What is it, who has it, and how did it evolve? *Science, 298*(5598), 1569–1579. https://doi.org/10.1126/science.298.5598.1569

Hockett, C. (1967). *The state of the art*. The Hague: Mouton.

Hockett, C. F. (1960). The origin of speech. *Scientific American, 203*, 88–96. https://doi.org/10.1038/scientificamerican0960-88

Hoffman, C. (1995). *An introduction to bilingualism*. Boston, MA: Addison Wesley Publishing Company.

Hornstein, N., & Lightfoot, D. (1981). Introduction. In N. Hornstein & D. Lightfoot (Eds.), *Explanation in linguistics: The logical problem of language acquisition* (pp. 9–31). New York: Longman.

Hout, R., Hulk, A., Kuiken, F., & Towell, R. J. (2003). *The lexicon–syntax interface in second language acquisition*. Amsterdam: John Benjamins. https://doi.org/10.1075/lald.30

Ingram, D. (1989). *First language acquisition: Method, description and explanation*. New York: Cambridge University Press.

IowaPrimate.LearningSanctuary (2010). *The amazing apes* [YouTube clip]. Retrieved from www.youtube.com/watch?v=HiWDKXRzSmU

Jessen, M., & Roux, J. C. (2002). Voice quality differences associated with stops and clicks in Xhosa. *Journal of Phonetics, 30*(1) 1–52. https://doi.org/10.1006/jpho.2001.0150

Jusczyk, P. W, & Hohne, E. A. (1997). Infants' memory for spoken words. *Science, 277*(5334), 1984–1986. https://doi.org/10.1126/science.277.5334.1984

Kanno, K. (2009). The stability of UG principles in second language acquisition: Evidence from Japanese. *Linguistics 36*, 1125–1146.

Kegl, J. (2002). Language emergence in a language-ready brain: Acquisition. In G. Morgan & B. Woll (Eds.), *Directions in sign language acquisition* (pp. 207–254). Amsterdam: John Benjamins. https://doi.org/10.1075/tilar.2.12keg

Kirman, P. (2007). *Screaming Goeldi's monkey* [YouTube clip]. Retrieved from www.youtube.com/watch?v=tWyBm3NzFOo

kissmycats3093. (2009). *This is me speaking in Pig Latin* [YouTube clip]. Retrieved from www.youtube.com/watch?v=FTnZFfjxbWs&feature=related

Klima, E. S., & Bellugi, U. (1966). Syntactic regularities in the speech of children. In J. Lyons & R. J. Wales (Eds.), *Psycholinguistic papers* (pp. 183–208). Edinburgh: Edinburgh University Press.

Kramer, S., Miller, D. A., & Newberger, J. (2009). *The linguists* [Documentary film]. USA: Ironbbound Films.

Lanehart, S. (2015). *Oxford handbook of African American language.* Oxford: Oxford University Press.

Larsen-Freeman, D., & Long, M. H. (1991). *An introduction to second language research.* London: Longman.

Leopold, W. (1949). *Speech development of a bilingual child: A linguist's record.* Evanston, IL: Northwestern University Studies in the Humanities.

Levine, L. E., & Munsch, J. (2013). *Child development: An active learning approach.* Thousand Oaks, CA: SAGE.

Lieberman, P. (2017, July 7). Comment on "Monkey vocal tracts are speech-ready". *Science Advances, 3*(7), e1700442. https://doi.org/10.1126/sciadv.1700442.

Lightfoot, D. (1982). *The language lottery: Toward a biology of grammar.* Cambridge, MA: MIT Press.

Lobeck, A. (1995). *Ellipsis: Functional heads, licensing and identification.* Oxford: Oxford University Press.

Logan, K. J. (2015). Fluency disorders. San Diego, CA: Plural Publishing.

Long, M., & Ross, V. (2011, November 18). Discover interview: The radical linguist Noam Chomsky. *Discover Magazine.* Retrieved from http://discovermagazine.com/2011/nov/18-discover-interview-radical-linguist-noam-chomsky.

Lowth, R. (1762). *A short introduction to English grammar.* Menston (Yorks): Scolar Press.

Lyiscott, J. (2014). *Broken English* [TED talk]. Retrieved from www.ted.com/talks/jamila_lyiscott_3_ways_to_speak_english

Malone, J. P. (2010). *The Kelloggs, Donald, and Gua* [YouTube clip]. Retrieved from www.youtube.com/watch?v=gCxf7yUDzio

Marcus, G. (2012, December 6). Happy Birthday, Noam Chomsky. *The New Yorker.* Retrieved from https://www.newyorker.com/news/news-desk/happy-birthday-noam-chomsky.

Marler, P. (1970). A comparative approach to vocal learning: Song development in white-crowned sparrows. *Journal of Comparative and Physiological Psychology, 71*(2, Pt.2), 1–25. https://doi.org/10.1037/h0029144

Marsh, J. (2011). *Project Nim* [Documentary film]. England: Red Box Films.

Masataka, N. (1992). Motherese in signed language. *Infant Behavior and Development, 15*(4), 453–460.

McNeill, D. (1966). Developmental psycholinguistics. In F. Smith & G. A. Miller (Eds.), *The genesis of language: A psycholinguistic approach.* Cambridge, MA: MIT Press.

Morin, O. (2016). *How traditions live and die*. New York: Oxford University Press.

Nevins, A., Pesetsky, D., & Rodrigues, C. (2009a). Pirahã exceptionality: A reassessment. *Language, 85*(2), 355–404. https://doi.org/10.1353/lan.0.0107

Nevins, A., Pesetsky, D., & Rodrigues, C. *(2009b)*. Evidence and argumentation: A reply to Everett (2009). *Language, 85*(3), 671–681. https://doi.org/10.1353/lan.0.0140

Newport, E. L. (1975). *Motherese: The speech of mothers to young children* (Ph.D. dissertation). University of Pennsylvania.

Newport, E. L. (1977). The speech of mothers to young children. In N. J. Castellan, D. B. Pisoni, & G. Potts (Eds.), *Cognitive theory* (Vol. 2). Hillsdale, NJ: Erlbaum.

Ochs, E. (1982). Talking to children in Western Samoa. *Language in Society, 11*(1), 77–104. https://doi.org/10.1017/S0047404500009040

The Onion. (2010). *Scientists successfully teach gorilla it will die someday* [TouTube clip]. Retrieved from www.youtube.com/watch?v=CJkWS4t4lok

Padilla, A.M., & Liebman, E. (1975). Language acquisition in the bilingual child. *The Bilingual Review/LaRevista Bilingue, 2*, 35–45.

Phillips, D. (2016, December 22). Photographer captures images of uncontacted Amazon tribe. *The Guardian*. Retrieved from https://www.theguardian.com/world/2016/dec/22/photographer-shows-first-images-of-uncontacted-amazon-tribe

Phillips, R. S. C. (1994). *Infant-directed speech in African American mothers* (Ph.D. dissertation). University of Illinois at Urbana-Champaign.

Pinker, S. (1994). *The language instinct*. New York: William Morrow and Company.

Pullum, G. (1999). African-American Vernacular English is not Standard English with mistakes. In S. Wheeler (Ed.), *The workings of language* (39–58) Westport, CT: Praeger.

Pye, C. (1983). Mayan telegraphese: Intonational determinants of inflectional development in Quiché Mayan. *Language, 59*, 583–604.

Radford, A. (2016). *Analysing English sentences*. Cambridge: Cambridge University Press. https://doi.org/10.1017/CBO9780511980312

Raffaele, P. (2006, November). Speaking Bonobo. *Smithsonian Magazine*. Retrieved from https://www.smithsonianmag.com/science-nature/speaking-bonobo-134931541/.

Ratner, N. B., & Pye, C. (1984). Higher pitch in BT is not universal: Acoustic evidence from Quiche Mayan. *Journal of Child Language, 11*(3), 515–522. https://doi.org/10.1017/S0305000900005924

Rickford, J. (1999). *The Ebonics controversy in my back yard: A sociolinguist's experiences and reflections. Journal of Sociolinguistics, 3(2), 267–275.* https://doi.org/10.1111/1467-9481.00076

Rickford, J R., & National Council of Teachers of English. (2013). *African American, Creole, and other vernacular Englishes in education: A bibliographic resource.* New York: Routledge.

Rymer, R. (1994). *Secret of the wild child* [Documentary film]. USA: Nova.

Sacks, O. (1998). *The man who mistook his wife for a hat.* New York: Simon and Schuster.

Said, E. (1999). *Out of place: A memoir.* New York: Random House.

Santiago, B. (2008). *Pardon my Spanglish.* Philadelphia: Quirk Books.

Salis, C. (2006). Comprehension of Wh-questions and declarative sentences in agrammatic aphasia (PhD dissertation). University of Reading.

Sauerland U. (2010). *Experimental evidence for complex syntax in Pirahã.* Unpublished manuscript, ZAS Berlin. Retrieved from www.zas.gwz-berlin.de/574.html.

Saville-Troike, M., & Barto, K. (2017). *Introducing second language acquisition.* Cambridge: Cambridge University Press.

Schieffelin, B. B. (1994). *How Kaluli children learn what to say, what to do, and how to feel.* New York: Cambridge University Press.

Schieffelin, B. B., & Ochs, E. (Eds.). (1987). *Language socialization across cultures.* Cambridge: Cambridge University Press. https://doi.org/10.1017/CBO9780511620898

Schwartz, B. D. (1999). Let's make up your mind: "Special nativist" perspectives on language, modularity of mind, and nonnative language acquisition. *Studies in Second Language Acquisition, 21*(4), 635–655. https://doi.org/10.1017/S0272263199004052

Searchinger, G. (1995). *The human language series* [Documentary film series]. England: Equinox Films.

Senghas, R. J., Senghas, A., & Pyers, J. E. (2005). The emergence of Nicaraguan sign language: Questions of development, acquisition, and evolution. In S. T. Parker, J. Langer, & C. Milbrath (Eds.), *Biology and knowledge revisited: From neurogenesis to psychogenesis* (pp. 287–306). London: Lawrence Erlbaum Associates.

Shneidman, L. A., & Goldin-Meadow, S. (2012). Language input and acquisition in a Mayan village: How important is directed speech? *Developmental Science, 15*(5), 659–673. https://doi.org/10.1111/j.1467-7687.2012.01168.x

Skinner, B. F. (1957). *Verbal behavior.* East Norwalk, CT: Appleton-Century-Crofts. https://doi.org/10.1037/11256-000

Smith, N., & Tsimpli, I. (1995). *The mind of a savant: Language, learning, and modularity*. Cambridge: Blackwell.

Snow, C. E. (1972). Mothers' speech to children learning language. *Child Development, 43*(2), 549–565.

Snow, C. E., & Ferguson, C. (1977). *Talking to children: Language input and acquisition: Papers from a Conference Sponsored by the Committee on Sociolinguistics of the Social Science Research Council (USA)*. Cambridge: Cambridge University Press.

Terrace, H. S., Petitto, L. A., Sanders, R. J., & Bever, T. G. (1979, November 23). Can an ape create a sentence? *Science, 206*(4421), 891–902.

Tinbergen, N. (1953). *The herring gull's world*. London: Collins.

Trask, R. L. (1999). *Key concepts in language and linguistics*. London: Routledge.

Trehub, S. (1976). The discrimination of foreign speech contrasts by infants and adults. *Child Development, 47*(2), 466–472. https://doi.org/10.2307/1128803

Uomini, N. T., & Meyer, G. F. (2013). Shared brain lateralization patterns in language and Acheulean stone tool production: A functional transcranial doppler ultrasound study. *PLOS ONE, 8*(8). https://doi.org/10.1371/journal.pone.0072693

Uriagereka, J. (1998). *Rhyme and reason: An introduction to minimalist syntax*. Cambridge: MIT Press.

Villeneuve, D. (Director) (2016). *Arrival* [Motion picture]. USA: Xenolinguistics.

Volterra, V., & Taeschner, T. (1978). The acquisition and development of language by bilingual children. *Journal of Child Language, 5*(2), 311–326. https://doi.org/10.1017/S0305000900007492

Walton, G. E., Bower, N. J. A., & Bower, T. G. R. (1992). Recognition of familiar faces by newborns. *Infant Behavior and Development, 15*, 265–269.

wash001. (2009). *Psychclips* [YouTube clip]. Retrieved from www.youtube.com/watch?v=OUwOvF7TqgA

Werker, J. (1989). Becoming a native listener. *American Scientist, 77*(1), 54–59.

Werker, J. (2014). *The baby human—Werker—ba/da study* [YouTube clip]. Retrieved from www.youtube.com/watch?v=Ew5-xbc1HMk&feature=related

Werker, J., & Tees, R. C. (1984). Cross-language speech perception: Evidence for perceptual reorganization during the first year of life. *Infant Behavior and Development, 7*(1), 49–63. https://doi.org/10.1016/S0163-6383(84)80022-3

White, L. (1985). The "pro-drop" parameter in adult second language learning. *Language Learning, 35*(1), 47–62. https://doi.org/10.1111/j.1467-1770.1985.tb01014.x

Wright, M. (2011). On clicks in English talk-in-interaction. *Journal of the International Phonetic Association, 41*(2), 207–229. https://doi.org/10.1017/S0025100311000144

Yun, S.-W. (2005). *The socializing role of codes and code-switching among Korean children in the United States* (Ph.D. dissertation). Oklahoma State University.

Zentella, A. C. (1997). *Growing up bilingual.* Oxford: Wiley-Blackwell.

Zimmer, B. (2004). "A Misattribution No Longer to be Put Up With". Posting date: December 12. Retrieved from http://itre.cis.upenn.edu/~myl/languagelog/archives/001715.html

Zimmer, B. (2005). "Churchill vs. Editorial Nonsense". Posting date: November 27. Retrieved from http://itre.cis.upenn.edu/~myl/languagelog/archives/002670.html

Index